Contents

You will have to think about the different points of view covered in this book and come to your own conclusions about the issues

Introduction

This book is written particularly for GCSE students studying either or both the AQA Religious Studies Specification B, Module 1 ('Thinking about God and Morality'), and/or Module 4 ('Truth, Spirituality and Contemporary Issues').

The first half of this book, Units 1–9, covers Module 1 of the exam: Thinking about God and Morality. The second half of the book, Units 10–16, covers Module 4: Truth, Spirituality and Contemporary Issues. You may be studying both of these modules as a full course GCSE, or you may be just studying one as a short course GCSE: your teacher can tell you which you are doing if you are not sure.

Different perspectives

An important part of your course is about comparing different viewpoints on issues. For your exam, you will be asked questions on the moral issues you will have studied and you will need to write about the viewpoints of two religious traditions on these moral issues.

This book looks at the issues from your course from the Christian perspective. Within Christianity there are many different Christian traditions: the Catholic Church, Church of England, Methodists, Society of Friends, etc. If you follow this book in your course, you will be comparing two Christian traditions when you study different moral issues.

Using examples

In your exam, you will be expected to include actual examples that are relevant to the question. You will need to use illustrations and examples from the teachings of your different religious traditions as well as different interpretations of religious writings.

Different Christian Traditions

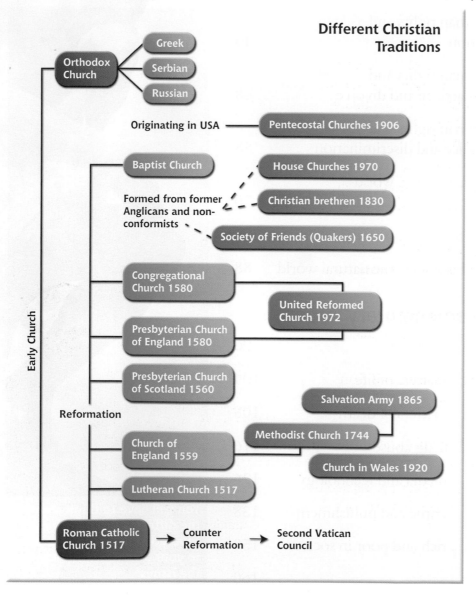

The moral issues in both parts of this book are often in the news, or featured in TV programmes. Look out for stories in the news about the moral issues – euthanasia, war and peace, crime, and all the other issues relevant to your course. Try and build up some case studies on particular issues so you have specific examples to use as evidence in your exam answers. The Internet also has many sites related to each of the moral issues in this book, which can help you find out more and keep up to date. Be careful about biased viewpoints on websites, however, and follow your teacher's guidance on using the Internet.

Examiners' tips

When your examiner marks your exam papers, he or she will be looking for particular things. Here are six things examiners will be looking for – whether you are answering questions on Thinking about God and Morality or Truth, Spirituality and Contemporary Issues. The examiner will be hoping you show that:

- you have knowledge and understanding of relevant teachings from sacred texts, religious leaders, religious organisations and non-religious groups and organisations, and that you can evaluate these

- you have knowledge and understanding of the different viewpoints which may exist within religious traditions and you can evaluate these

- you have knowledge and understanding of significant secular (non-religious) responses related to the moral issues studied and you can evaluate these secular responses

- you have knowledge and understanding of the legal position related to each of the moral issues studied and you can evaluate the legal position

- you appreciate the relationship between religious beliefs and teachings and the way in which believers live their lives

- you can evaluate the different viewpoints and teachings related to each issue that you have presented, and that you have set out your personal response to the issue.

Activity

Choose one Christian tradition from the chart opposite. Using the Internet and/or the library:

1 find out how it came to be formed

2 write a brief description of the major Christian beliefs of this tradition

3 write a description of how Christians organise worship in this tradition.

How do we prove things exist?

Is this a genuine UFO or trick photography?

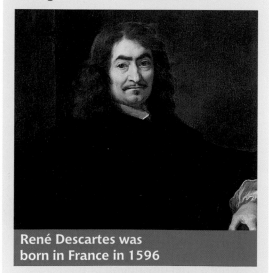

René Descartes was born in France in 1596

What is...?

Logic is to work things out using a chain of reasoning to reach a conclusion.

There are **three** main ways by which the existence of things is proved. The first is personal experience – 'I have seen it, so I know it exists.' The second is reliable evidence – 'I have not seen it but other people have convinced me that they have.' The third is **logic** – 'I have not seen it but there are logical reasons to believe in it.' The three types of evidence can be demonstrated by looking at how people prove the existence of aliens from outer space. People who accept that aliens exist would use one or all of the following types of proof.

- They are certain aliens exist because they have seen them for themselves.

- They accept as genuine the accounts and evidence given by other people of sightings of aliens.

- It does not seem that with the millions of planets that exist in the universe, there is only life on earth, so it is logical to accept life exists on other planets.

Other people refuse to accept the evidence people give to prove things. For example, people reject the existence of aliens from outer space because they:

- have not seen any evidence of alien life for themselves so do not accept aliens exist.

- do not accept the evidence of sightings by other people as sufficient proof. They think that the people who claim to have seen aliens might be hallucinating or lying. It might be a case of mistaken identity (for example, some people have mistaken weather balloons for UFOs), or a deliberate hoax to fool people.

- think that without any proof of life on other planets it is not logical to accept the existence of aliens.

How do we prove God exists?

The same type of evidence that is used to prove or reject the existence of aliens from outer space can be used to prove or reject the existence of God. A **theist** is certain that God exists because they:

- are certain that they have been in contact with God directly, or
- accept the accounts that other people have given of their experience of God as evidence that God exists, or
- believe that God is the only logical explanation for the origin of the universe and the order within it.

An **atheist** rejects any belief in God, as they do not believe that any evidence accepted by theists is sufficient proof that God exists.

An **agnostic** believes that any evidence produced by theists does not prove the existence of God one way or the other.

What do you think? ?

- Do you think that you are a theist, an atheist, or an agnostic?
- Discuss the reasons for your view with your teacher and the rest of the class.

Questions ?

- Explain **three** different types of evidence people use to prove things exist.
- Explain why other people might reject these forms of evidence as proof of existence.
- Explain the difference between a theist and an atheist.
- 'There is no evidence that God exists.' Do you agree? Give reasons for your answer, showing that you have thought about more than one point of view.

What is...?

A **theist** is someone who believes in the existence of God (or gods).

An **atheist** is someone who does not believe in the existence of God (or gods).

An **agnostic** believes that it is impossible to know if God (or gods) exist.

Activity

Divide the class into four groups. Each group represents one of the following people: a theist who attends a place of worship regularly, a person who believes in God but does not attend a place of worship, an atheist and an agnostic. Each group is to work out reasons the person would give for their beliefs. Try to support your group's points with **empirical evidence** and **persuasive evidence**.

A representative from each group is to come to the front of the class to form part of a 'Question Time' panel to discuss whether or not God exists. There needs to be a chairperson to control the discussion. Each member of the panel is to state their views and then members of the class can ask the panel questions about their beliefs or add additional points to support or reject a view expressed by the panel.

What is...?

Empirical evidence is evidence that is proved through scientific experiment or people see it for themselves.

Persuasive evidence is evidence that results in a person accepting a belief but it may not be something that can be experienced or measured by scientific experiment.

How do we prove God exists? 1

The First Cause argument

Some theists would use the existence of the universe to prove the existence of God. They would argue:

- things exist because they are caused to exist
- the universe exists so it was caused to exist
- the cause of the universe was God.

This is called the First Cause argument. It is given this name because it is arguing that the first cause of the universe was God.

St Thomas Aquinas was a Christian who lived in the Middle Ages. He said that things could not cause themselves to come into existence so something had to cause them. The universe exists and so must have been caused by something outside the universe. St Thomas Aquinas argued that this first cause of the universe was God.

Was God the first cause of the universe?

Questions ?

- What is the First Cause argument?
- Why do you think many Christians use Genesis 1–2:3 to support the First Cause argument?

What is...? 📖

Genesis is the first book of the Christian Bible. The word 'genesis' means 'origin'. Genesis contains an account of the creation (origin) of the universe by God. Many Christians believe that the First Cause argument is supported by Genesis 1–2:3.

What was the first cause of the universe?

The creation account (Genesis 1–2:3)

In the beginning, when God created the universe, the earth was formless and desolate. The raging ocean that covered everything was engulfed in total darkness, and the Spirit of God was moving over the water. Then God commanded, 'Let there be light' – and light appeared. God was pleased with what he saw. Then he separated the light from the darkness and he named the light 'Day' and the darkness 'Night'. Evening passed and morning came – that was the first day.

Then God commanded, 'Let there be a dome to divide the water and to keep it in two separate places' – and it was done. So God made a dome, and it separated the water under it from the water above it. He named the dome 'Sky'. Evening passed and morning came – that was the second day.

Then God commanded, 'Let the water below the sky come together in one place, so that the land will appear' – and it was done. He named the land 'Earth', and the water which had come together he named 'Sea'. And God was pleased with what he saw. Then he commanded, 'Let the earth produce all kinds of plants, those that bear grain and those that bear fruit' – and it was done. So the earth produced all kinds of plants, and God was pleased with what he saw. Everything passed and morning came – that was the third day.

Then God commanded, 'Let lights appear in the sky to separate day from night and to show the time when days, years, and religious festivals begin; they will shine in the sky to give light to the earth – and it was done. So God made the two larger lights, the sun to rule over the day and the moon to rule over the night; he also made the stars. He placed the lights in the sky to shine on the earth, to rule over the day and the night, and to separate light from darkness. And God was pleased with what he saw. Evening passed and morning came – that was the fourth day.

Then God commanded, 'Let the water be filled with many kinds of living beings, and let the air be filled with birds.' So God created the great sea monsters, all kinds of creatures that live in the water, and all kinds of birds. And God was pleased with what he saw. He blessed them all and told the creatures that live in the water to reproduce, and to fill the sea, and he told the birds to increase in number. Evening passed and morning came – that was the fifth day.

Then God commanded, 'Let the earth produce all kinds of animal life: domestic and wild, large and small' – and it was done. So God made them all, and he was pleased with what he saw.

Then God said, 'And now we will make human beings; they will be like us and resemble us. They will have power over the fish, the birds, and all animals, domestic and wild, large and small.' So God created human beings, making them to be like himself. He created them male and female, blessed them, and said, 'Have many children, so that your descendants will live all over the earth and bring it under their control. I am putting you in charge of the fish, the birds, and all the wild animals. I have provided all kinds of grain and all kinds of fruit for you to eat; but for all the wild animals and for all the birds I have provided grass and leafy plants for food' – and it was done. God looked at everything he had made, and he was very pleased. Evening passed and morning came – that was the sixth day.

And so the whole universe was completed. By the seventh day God finished what he had been doing and stopped working. He blessed the seventh day and set it apart as a special day, because by that day he had completed his creation and stopped working.

How do we prove God exists? 2

Did the universe begin with the Big Bang?

Activity

1 Using the Internet and/or library, find out more about the scientific theory known as the Big Bang.

2 Outline the Big Bang theory in your own words.

Activity

Try to imagine that you do not know the purpose of a watch. Look at the stone and the watch in the picture and write down the differences between them. What would you be able to tell about the watch, even if you did not know what it was used for? How is the watch different from the stone?

When you have finished, share your thoughts with your teacher and the rest of the class.

What are the differences between a stone and a watch?

The Big Bang theory

A challenge science has made to the First Cause argument is the Big Bang theory. This is a scientific theory that explains the beginning of the universe about 15 billion years ago from an initial point in the past, known as the 'Big Bang'. Scientists do not know what existed before the Big Bang, but many think that there was nothing – no space, no time: nothing.

Many theists would use the Big Bang theory to support the First Cause argument and say that the 'Big Bang' is how God caused the universe to exist. Atheists often use the theory to reject the existence of God and argue that the Big Bang proves that the universe resulted from a random event not an action by God, and that religious accounts of creation are just myths.

The Design argument

The Design argument states that the universe is too ordered and complicated to have come about by random chance, therefore it must have been designed. A design needs a designer. The designer of the universe is God. Most Christians believe that the Genesis account of creation supports the Design argument as it shows that God planned the stages of development of the world.

St Thomas Aquinas said that things could only be kept in regular order by an intelligent being; the planets, sun, moon and stars rotate in the universe in a set pattern because God keeps them in their place. When Isaac Newton discovered the existence of gravity, religious believers such as William Paley saw this as part of God's design to keep the regular movement of the heavenly bodies.

William Paley, an eighteenth century English philosopher, used the Design argument to prove the existence of God. Paley argued that if we found a watch, even if we did not know its function, we would know that there is evidence of design. In the same way, if we look at the natural world, we can tell that there is evidence of design. Paley used the example of things that are just right for their purpose, such as the eye for sight, birds' wings for flight, and fish gills for breathing under water. He argued that things that are designed need a designer. The designer of the world he believed was God.

Isaac Newton used the fact that we all have individual patterns on our thumbs as evidence that God has planned each human separately.

The theory of evolution

Many atheists use Darwin's theory of evolution to account for apparent design in the world instead of God. Darwin argued that a random variation in a plant or animal might help it to survive better than other members of the species. This variation would be inherited by future generations and eventually be found in all members of the species as they adapt to their environment. He called this process 'natural selection'. These changes are called evolution.

Atheists such as the zoologist Richard Dawkins argue that it is evolution that has given the appearance of design, not God. He argues that the variations in the world are caused by random changes in the DNA molecules of any life form and not by a designer God. The existence of natural suffering and the cruelty found within nature are evidence that the world is not designed.

The Anthropic Principle is a modern version of the Design argument. Some theists argue that God planned (designed) the world so that eventually human life would develop, and God brought this about through the process of evolution. They argue that if humans had evolved by random chance then they would not need to write books, paint pictures, or create music to survive. The fact that humans can do these things suggests that we are designed and for a believer this designer is God.

Is the ability to paint necessary for survival?

Activity

1 Using the Internet and/or library, find out more about Richard Dawkins' views.

2 Use your research to explain why Richard Dawkins wrote a book called *The Blind Watchmaker*.

Questions ?

1 (a) Explain the Big Bang theory.
  (b) Explain how an atheist might use the Big Bang theory to reject the existence of God.
  (c) Explain how a theist might use the Big Bang theory to support the existence of God.
2 Explain in your own words the Design argument of St Thomas Aquinas and William Paley.
3 (a) Explain the theory of evolution.
  (b) Explain how an atheist might use the theory of evolution to reject the existence of God.
  (c) Explain how a theist might use the theory of evolution to support the existence of God.
4 'The Big Bang theory and the theory of evolution have led to the rejection of the Genesis account of creation.' Do you agree? Give reasons for your answer, showing that you have thought about more than one point of view. Refer to religious teachings in your answer.

Religious experience 1

What is...?

Prayer is both talking and listening to God.

Meditation is to focus the mind on a specific subject, in the case of a believer this will be God.

What is...?

Charismatic worship happens when some Christians believe that during the service the Holy Spirit is working in members of the congregation. The Holy Spirit is believed by Christians to be the part of God that works in the world today.

Sacramental worship happens when it is believed by some Christians that in the service there is an outward sign of an inner gift from God.

So far we have looked at the fact that some theists try to prove the existence of God through the natural world. Experiencing something directly is usually the strongest form of proof for an individual. Some theists are certain that God exists because they claim to have experienced God. When people claim to have met God personally, this is called a religious experience and it can take many forms. Religious experiences that Christians may claim to have had include:

- communicating with God through prayer and meditation
- feeling God's presence in worship
- feeling the presence of God in nature
- experiencing a conversion
- a miraculous event.

Communicating with God through prayer and meditation

When they pray, a believer is not only speaking to God but also listening for God's reply. During such times, believers say they have felt the presence of God. Some worshippers meditate to feel closer to God. Some Christians will withdraw from everyday life and 'go on retreat' to give their full attention to God.

Charismatic worship is spontaneous, as the believers feel moved by the Holy Spirit

Feeling God's presence in worship

Christians may feel God's presence in worship as either a **charismatic** event or in **sacramental worship** such as Holy Communion.

Pentecostal worship is an example of Christian worship in which there may be a charismatic event. Pentecostalists believe that the gifts of the Holy Spirit are available to the faithful and it is through these gifts that they experience God. A Pentecostal service is very lively, with the congregation clapping and dancing 'in the spirit'. It does not have a fixed order of service and the worship is spontaneous. Worshippers raise their hands in the air as they praise and thank God for everything done for them.

Sometimes, members of the congregation may feel overwhelmed by God's Holy Spirit and they almost faint and fall on the floor. Other members of the congregation may 'speak in tongues' (glossolalia), as they feel so moved by the Holy Spirit that normal speech seems inadequate. To outsiders, it sounds like a jumble of sounds, but other members of the Church translate the sounds for the rest of the congregation. Other worshippers believe that they have the gift of prophecy and can 'hear' God's voice and say what it means. Sometimes, members of the Church appear to have the gift of healing and use these gifts to try and cure people of illness in faith healing services.

The Catholic Church is a Christian tradition that celebrates the sacrament of Holy Communion. They call this service the Mass. Catholics believe that when the priest dedicates the bread and wine to God it becomes the actual body and blood of Christ. These Christians believe that during the Mass Christ's sacrifice for the forgiveness of sins is repeated. The bread and wine are believed to be food and drink for the spiritual life of those taking part in the service, to gain eternal life and God's forgiveness. The service follows the same pattern each time so that whenever a Catholic attends the Mass they know what is happening, even if it is in a different language from their own. The Catholic Church teaches that when believers take the bread and wine they can be certain of the presence of Jesus and the existence of God.

What do you think? ?

The worship in the Pentecostal Church is spontaneous and differs from service to service. The worship in the Catholic Church follows a set pattern so that the form of the service is the same from week to week. Which of the two types of service do you think is more likely to result in the theist feeling the presence of God? Give reasons for your view in your answer.

Activity

1 List the gifts of the Holy Spirit that Pentecostalists believe can be received from God.

2 Explain how these 'gifts' might be used to prove God exists through religious experience.

Catholics believe that Christ is present in the bread and wine

Activity

Using the Internet and/or library, research one of the following forms of Holy Communion and write a detailed account of what happens during the service to show how the congregation might experience the presence of God.

• The Catholic Mass

• The Orthodox Divine Liturgy

• The Eucharist in the Church of England.

Religious experience 2

Some people feel the presence of God when looking at the beauty of nature

God in nature

Some theists are convinced that they have felt the presence of God while walking in the countryside because of feelings of **awe** and wonder they experience while looking at the beauty of nature.

Experiencing a conversion

Some theists believe that God has contacted them directly and as a result of this experience are converted to believe in God or to change their beliefs about God. An early Christian, St Paul, was originally a Jew who wanted to kill Christians. On his way to the city of Damascus he had a religious experience that converted him to Christianity.

A miraculous event

Other theists claim to have experienced God through a miraculous event. It may be that they or someone close to them has been cured of a terminal illness or disability and yet the doctors cannot explain how it has happened. It may be that they or someone close to them has been saved from certain death by a freak event.

The effect of a person's religious experience may not only cause them to believe that God exists but it may also cause others to believe as well. Although they have not had the religious experience directly, they accept that it is genuine and proof that God exists. After his conversion, Paul, as he became known, travelled around the Mediterranean spreading the Christian message and converting others to the faith. Many sick or handicapped Christians attend faith healing services because they hope for a miraculous cure.

Proof of God's existence?

The main problem in using religious experiences as proof of the existence of God is that they are difficult to prove as genuine.

What is...?

Awe is reverential feelings of fear or wonder.

Conversion is when a person changes his or her beliefs or religion.

Activity

1 Read the account of the conversion of St Paul. St Paul was called Saul before his conversion.

2 Imagine that you are Ananias and write a letter to the Christians in Jerusalem telling them what has happened and why they no longer need to fear Saul.

What is...?

A **miracle** is an extraordinary event, which seems to break the laws of nature. A miracle is considered to be an act of God.

What do you think? ?

- Why do you think that some people who experience a conversion say that they have had a 'Damascus road experience'?

St Paul's conversion (Acts 9:1–22)

In the meantime Saul kept up his violent threats of murder against the followers of the Lord. He went to the High Priest and asked for letters of introduction to the synagogues in Damascus, so that if he should find there any followers of the Way of the Lord, he would be able to arrest them, both men and women, and bring them back to Jerusalem.

As Saul was coming near the city of Damascus, suddenly a light from the sky flashed round him. He fell to the ground and heard a voice saying to him, 'Saul, Saul! Why do you persecute me?'

'Who are you, Lord?' he asked.

'I am Jesus, whom you persecute,' the voice said. 'But get up and go into the city, where you will be told what you must do.'

The men who were travelling with Saul had stopped, not saying a word; they heard the voice but could not see anyone. Saul got up from the ground and opened his eyes, but could not see a thing. So they took him by the hand and led him into Damascus. For three days he was not able to see, and during that time he did not eat or drink anything.

There was a believer in Damascus named Ananias. He had a vision, in which the Lord said to him, 'Ananias!'

'Here I am, Lord,' he answered.

The Lord said to him, 'Get ready and go to Straight Street, and at the house of Judas ask for a man from Tarsus named Saul. He is praying, and in a vision he has seen a man named Ananias come in and place his hands on him so that he might see again.'

Ananias answered, 'Lord, many people have told me about this man and about all the terrible things he has done to your people in Jerusalem. And he has come to Damascus with authority from the chief priests to arrest all who worship you.'

The Lord said to him, 'Go, because I have chosen him to serve me, to make my name known to Gentiles and kings and to the people of Israel.

And I myself will show him all that he must suffer for my sake.'

So Ananais went, entered the house where Saul was, and placed his hands on him. 'Brother Saul,' he said, 'the Lord has sent me – Jesus himself, who appeared to you on the road as you were coming here. He sent me so that you might see again and be filled with the Holy Spirit.' At once something like fish scales fell from Saul's eyes, and he was able to see again. He stood up and was baptised; and after he had eaten, his strength came back.

Saul stayed for a few days with the believers in Damascus. He went straight to the synagogues and began to preach that Jesus was the Son of God.

All who heard him were amazed and asked, 'Isn't he the one who in Jerusalem was killing those who worship that man Jesus? And didn't he come here for the very purpose of arresting those people and taking them back to the chief priests?'

But Saul's preaching became even more powerful, and his proofs that Jesus was the Messiah were so convincing that the Jews who lived in Damascus could not answer him.

The only evidence for people who have not had the experience is the effect on the individual claiming to have experienced God.

Atheists do not accept religious experiences as proof of the existence of God. They believe that the person is mistaken or misled. The person might have imagined the experience because they wanted to believe God exists or claimed that an ordinary experience is religious. Miracles are no more than coincidences. For example, an atheist would say that a parachutist who survived after his parachute did not open, did so by chance and not by a miracle.

Questions ?

1 (a) Explain what is meant by a religious experience.
  (b) State and explain **four** examples of religious experience.
2 What reasons would atheists give for rejecting religious experiences?

Evil and suffering 1

Floods are an example of natural evil

We talk about evil as being the cause of suffering. There are two types of evil.

- Moral evil refers to human actions that cause suffering to others. Examples of moral evil are murder, rape, war, cruelty and dishonesty. Moral evil is 'man-made' evil.

- Natural evil refers to events that are not the result of human action but still cause suffering. These are natural events such as earthquakes, volcanic eruptions, flooding, illness and death.

The attributes of God

Many atheists argue that the existence of evil and suffering in the world is evidence that God does not exist, especially as much of the suffering appears unfair. It is often good and innocent people who suffer, while sometimes nothing unpleasant seems to happen to others who are selfish and cruel. St Thomas Aquinas recognised that this was a problem that a believer had to address: if God is good then how can God and evil both exist?

God is often described as 'all-loving', 'all-knowing' and 'all powerful' – there is no limit to his power, he knows everything and he loves everyone without exception and completely. A question often asked by both theists and atheists is, 'If God is all-loving, all-knowing and all-powerful, why is there evil and suffering in the world?' The eighteenth century philosopher David Hume argued that God could not be all three.

- Either God is all-loving and all-knowing but does not have the *power* to stop the evil, or

- God is all-loving and all-powerful but does not *know* there is evil in the world, or

- God is all-powerful and all-knowing but does not *love* us enough to stop the evil.

If God does not have all three attributes (qualities) then it would make God very different from the God that Christians believe in. The nineteenth century philosopher John Stuart Mill challenged the idea that the world was designed by God. Mill argued that a God that is all-knowing, all-loving and all-powerful would design a perfect world. The cruelty in nature, the natural evils like volcanoes or floods, the moral evil of humans, were all proof, he said, that this world is far from perfect. That meant that it could not have been designed by an all-knowing, all-loving and all-powerful God.

A theist has to find a solution to the problem of the existence of evil and suffering and at the same time keep the belief in an all-loving, all-powerful (omniscient) and all-knowing (omnipotent) God.

Christian explanations

Christians seek to either remove the blame for the existence of evil and suffering in the world from God, or to find a purpose for the existence of evil and suffering. Christian explanations for the existence of evil and suffering include:

- the 'work of the devil'
- the result of God allowing humans to have **free will**
- the result of external influences
- a test of faith
- the punishment for **sin**.

The 'work of the devil'

Satan is another name for the devil. For some Christians, the devil is an actual being. They believe Satan was an angel who rebelled against God and as a punishment was thrown out of heaven. Satan tries to tempt people to turn away from God. The evil comes from humans giving in to the temptations he offers.

Other Christians may use the phrase 'work of the devil' to refer to all that is evil in the world, but do not believe that Satan is an actual being. For them, evil and the suffering that comes from it is due to the faults in our society. For example, someone may commit an evil action because they have never been taught right from wrong as a child. These Christians see evil as an impersonal force and say Satan is not real but just a colourful way of describing how people feel tempted to do things they know are wrong.

The misuse of free will

Some Christians look at the account of the **Fall** in Genesis 3 as an explanation of how evil and suffering came into the world. When God created humans, God gave them the free will to either love and serve him, or to disobey him. The first humans, Adam and Eve, abused this freedom and disobeyed God in the Garden of Eden when they were tempted by the snake (Satan) to eat from the Tree of the Knowledge of Good and Evil; as a result of this **original sin**, evil came into the world. Adam and Eve were thrown out of the Garden of Eden and pain and suffering came into the world.

Why did God not stop the aeroplanes crashing into the World Trade Centre?

Questions ?

1 Explain the **two** types of evil found in the world.
2 What problem does the existence of apparent evil and suffering in the world cause for a believer?
3 Explain **two** different understandings of the term 'work of the devil' that Christians might have.
4 What is meant by 'free will'?
5 'There is no such thing as evil.' Do you agree? Give reasons for your answer, showing that you have thought about more than one point of view.

Evil and suffering 2

God tested the faith of Job through suffering

Activity

1 Read the account of the Fall opposite.

2 In your own words, explain the origin of evil and suffering as described in the Genesis account of the Fall.

Questions ?

1 Outline and explain **three** different explanations for the existence of evil and suffering found in Christianity.
2 'The fact that people suffer has nothing to do with God.' Do you agree? Give reasons for your answer, showing that you have thought about more than one point of view.

Some Christians believe that the Fall was a real event and all human beings have inherited the original sin of Adam and Eve, to which each person adds their own sins. Other Christians say the Fall is a story that teaches people the consequences of using our free will to turn away from God. These Christians argue that when humans disobey God evil is brought into the world. Jesus came into the world to show people how to use their free will to live as God would wish and to overcome evil and suffering. Jesus was tempted by Satan on several occasions but refused to give in to temptation.

Psychological reasons

Many people in our society believe that evil is a psychological phenomenon. In this argument, evil is caused by mental problems or influences. For example, many serial killers are psychotic. Other less dramatic evils in society could also have a psychological cause. For example, some people say society is more violent because of the influence of violent films and computer games on children's mind.

Test of faith

Most Christians believe that God will judge people on the way in which they have lived their lives according to his laws. Those who have lived as God would wish will go to heaven to be with God, whereas those who have ignored God will be separated from God. Some Christians believe that this judgement is only fair if an individual's faith has been tested through pain and suffering. If nothing went wrong in the world then there would be no way that people could show their trust and love of God. One example of such a test of faith is found in the Old Testament story of Job.

Some Christians argue that it is through pain and suffering that people learn the difference between right and wrong and how they should behave. Some Christians believe that every time we do the right thing our souls are strengthened and we draw closer to God, and every time we sin then the resulting evil and suffering is a deserved punishment for that sin.

God's plan

For some Christians, the answer lies in the fact that God is beyond human understanding. It is not possible for humans to understand God's plan for the world and therefore to explain why evil and suffering exist. It may be that evil and suffering is part of a good plan that God has for the world. These Christians would say that it is not for humans to question God but simply to trust in his goodness.

The Fall (Genesis 3)

Now the snake was the most cunning animal that the Lord God had made. The snake asked the woman, 'Did God really tell you not to eat fruit from any tree in the garden?'

'We may eat the fruit of any tree in the garden,' the woman answered, 'except the tree in the middle of it. God told us not to eat the fruit of that tree or even touch it; if we do, we will die.'

The snake replied, 'That's not true; you will not die. God said that, because he knows that when you eat it you will be like God and know what is good and what is bad.'

The woman saw how beautiful the tree was and how good its fruit would be to eat, and she thought how wonderful it would be to become wise. So she took some of the fruit and ate it. Then she gave some to her husband, and he also ate it. As soon as they had eaten it, they were given understanding and realised that they were naked; so they sewed fig leaves together and covered themselves.

That evening they heard the Lord God walking in the garden, and they hid from him among the trees. But the Lord God called out to the man, 'Where are you?'

He answered, 'I heard you in the garden; I was afraid and hid from you, because I was naked.'

'Who told you that you were naked?' God asked. 'Did you eat the fruit that I told you not to eat?'

The man answered, 'The woman you put here with me gave me the fruit, and I ate it.'

The Lord God asked the woman, 'Why did you do this?'

She replied, 'The snake tricked me into eating it.'

Then the Lord God said to the snake, 'You will be punished for this; you alone of all the animals must bear this curse: from now on you will have to crawl on your belly, and you will have to eat dust as long as you live. I will make you and the woman hate each other; her offspring and yours will always be enemies. Her offspring will crush your head, and you will bite her offspring's heel.'

And he said to the woman, 'I will increase your trouble in pregnancy and your pain in giving birth. In spite of this, you will still have desire for your husband, yet you will be subject to him.'

And he said to the man, 'You listened to your wife and ate the fruit which I told you not to eat.

Because of what you have done, the ground will be under a curse. You will have to work hard all your life to make it produce enough food for you. It will produce weeds and thorns, and you will have to eat wild plants. You will have to work hard and sweat to make the soil

produce anything, until you go back to the soil from which you were formed. You were made from soil, and you will become soil again.'

Adam named his wife Eve, because she was the mother of all human beings. And the Lord God made clothes out of animal skins for Adam and his wife, and he clothed them.

Then the Lord God said, 'Now the man has become like one of us and has knowledge of what is good and what is bad. He must not be allowed to take fruit from the tree that gives life, eat it, and live for ever. So the Lord God sent him out of the Garden of Eden and made him cultivate the soil from which he had been formed. Then at the east side of the garden he put living creatures and a flaming sword which turned in all directions. This was to keep anyone from coming near the tree that gives life.

what people believe about the existence of God?

The Blind Girl, John Everett Millais

Task 1

Read the following statements and then answer the questions that follow.

> **A:** *'God is a special kind of person that I can experience through prayer.'*
>
> **B:** *'God does not exist.'*
>
> **C:** *'God may exist but perhaps God does not exist.'*

1 **(a)** Which statement would be made by an atheist?

   (b) Complete the statement beginning: 'An atheist would say that…'

2 Explain what Statement A means, including what is meant by prayer.

3 **(a)** Which statement would be made by an agnostic?

   (b) Complete the statement beginning: 'An agnostic would say that…'

4 **(a)** What is a theist?

   (b) Complete the statement: 'A theist would say that…'

Task 2

1 Explain why it is hard to prove that God exists.

2 Explain how St Thomas Aquinas tried to prove that God exists.

3 Explain how atheists would argue against St Thomas Aquinas' argument.

Task 3

1 Explain the Design argument of William Paley.

2 Explain the Anthropic Principle.

3 Explain how atheists would argue against the Design argument, including the Anthropic Principle.

Task 4

1 Choose **three** different ways by which people might believe that they have experienced God.

2 'Religious experiences are just an illusion.' Do you agree? Give reasons for your answer, showing that you have thought about more than one point of view.

The temptation of Jesus (Matthew 4:1–11)

Then the spirit led Jesus into the desert to be tempted by the Devil. After spending 40 days and nights without food, Jesus was hungry. Then the Devil came to him and said, 'If you are God's Son, order these stones to turn into bread.'

But Jesus answered, 'The scripture says, "Human beings cannot live on bread alone, but need every word that God speaks."'

Then the Devil took Jesus to Jerusalem, the Holy City, set him on the highest point of the Temple, and said to him, 'If you are God's Son, throw yourself down, for the scripture says:

"God will give orders to his angels about you;

they will hold you up with their hands,

so that not even your feet will be hurt on the stones."'

Jesus answered, 'But the scripture also says, "Do not put the Lord your God to the test."'

Then the devil took Jesus to a very high mountain and showed him all the kingdoms of the world in all their greatness. 'All this I will give you,' the Devil said, 'if you kneel down and worship me.'

Then Jesus answered, 'Go away, Satan! The scripture says, "Worship the Lord your God and serve only him!"'

Then the Devil left Jesus; and angels came and helped him.

Task 5

The philosopher Immanuel Kant believed that we cannot know anything about things that we cannot experience through our five senses. The woman in the painting by John Everett Millais is blind.

1 What are the five senses by which Kant believed we experience things?

2 According to Kant's philosophy, what can the woman never experience because she is blind?

3 What can the woman still experience despite the fact that she is blind?

4 How do you think Kant's philosophy puts limits on proving things exist?

Task 6

The New Testament explains that Jesus was tempted by the devil to use his powers for himself. Read the passage above from Matthew 4:1–11 and answer the questions that follow.

1 Explain the **three** temptations of Jesus.

2 What did Jesus mean by his replies to the temptations?

3 What different understandings might Christians have of this incident?

4 'There is too much evil and suffering in the world for there to be an all-loving, all-powerful, all-knowing God.' Do you agree? Give reasons for your answer, showing that you have thought about more than one point of view.

Citizenship Link

In every society there are people who believe in God but do not worship God in the same way. There are other people who do not believe that God exists.

Design a questionnaire to find out what different beliefs about God are held in your area.

When you have completed your findings, convert them to a graph to show the different religious traditions in your area and the number of people who do not believe in God. You could use a computer spreadsheet program for this activity.

What is God like? 1

A polytheist believes that there are different gods and goddesses. An example of a religion that worshipped many gods existed in Ancient Egypt.

The Ancient Egyptian gods

Many of the Ancient Egyptian gods represented strong forces in the natural world such as the sun and the river Nile. Other gods were responsible for specific cities or had specific roles in the world. For example, the god Khnum, the ram-headed god, was believed to create humans on his potter's wheel. The Ancient Egyptians often portrayed their gods as animals. For example, they chose the hawk, which flies high in the sky, to represent the sun god, Horus.

The gods were worshipped in temples where sacrifices were offered to the gods. Actual images of the gods were at the centre of the worship, and festivals were held to celebrate the life and work of the gods. Living a good life was thought to be the way of ensuring a safe passage to the afterworld. A dead person's heart was weighed in a balance against a feather, which represented Truth. If the heart were lighter than the feather then the person would be allowed to enter the afterworld, but if it was heavier than the feather then the individual was destroyed forever.

What is...?

Monotheism is the belief in the existence of one God.

Polytheism is the belief in more than one God.

Activity

Using the Internet and/or the library, research one of the Egyptian gods or goddesses and write a paragraph to explain the Egyptian beliefs about the god or goddess you have chosen.

Many Egyptian gods had the body of a man or woman but the head of an animal or part of an animal as their head-dress

Monotheism

Believing that God has many forms is not the same as being a polytheist. Christians are monotheists and believe that God is one. Many Christians believe that there are three different aspects to God or sides to God's nature (the Trinity). These aspects of God are: God the Father, God the Son, God the Holy Spirit.

God the Father is the part of God in heaven, God the Son came to earth in the form of Jesus, and God the Holy Spirit is the part of God that works in the world.

The attributes of God in Christianity

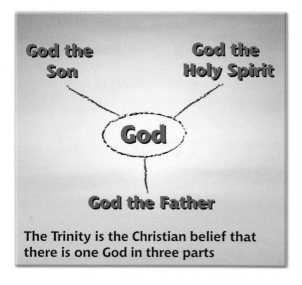

The Trinity is the Christian belief that there is one God in three parts

Questions ?

1 (a) Name a polytheistic religion.
  (b) What is polytheism?
2 (a) Name a monotheistic religion.
  (b) What is monotheism?
3 Explain the Christian understanding of the Trinity.
4 State and explain **four** of the attributes of God accepted by monotheists.
5 Explain the difference between a belief in a God that is personal from a belief in a God that is impersonal.
6 'There is only one God and it is wrong to think of God in different forms.' Do you agree? Give reasons for your answer, showing that you have thought about more than one point of view.

What is...?

Immanent is to believe that God is present in and involved with life on earth and in the universe.

Transcendent is to believe that God is beyond and outside life on earth and the universe. God is outside time and space and beyond human understanding.

Activity

1 Look back at the attributes of God on page 23.

2 Draw two columns in your book with the headings 'Transcendent' and 'Immanent'.

3 In the first column, list all the aspects (attributes) of God that match the idea of a transcendent God, and in the second column, list the aspects of God that match the idea of an immanent God.

Christians believe God became immanent in the form of Jesus

Is God personal or impersonal?

Christians believe that no other being has the power of God. For some Christians, Almighty God is **impersonal**. God the creator may be a force or power with whom it is not possible to have a personal relationship. Yet most Christians believe that it is possible to have a **personal** relationship with God. They believe that they can talk to God through prayer and listen to his reply.

Many Christians believe God has revealed himself as the perfect 'Father'. A father who loves and cares for his children, and wants the best for them but allows them the freedom to make mistakes and hopefully grow as a result. As a good father, God guides and disciplines his children. God will judge his 'children' on how they have lived by his rules and the relationship with God is therefore personal. For most Christians, God can be both personal and impersonal.

Is God immanent or transcendent?

To describe God as both **immanent** and **transcendent** seems to be opposing ways of describing God's nature. Most Christians believe that God is incomprehensible and outside time and space, and that God's power is unlimited. This is why Christians state that they believe in an Almighty God. Although God is believed to be transcendent, most Christians believe God is immanent because God has been, is, and will be, involved in the history of the world. Christians believe God became immanent in the form of Jesus to show people how he wanted people to live according to his will. God remains immanent through the action of the Holy Spirit. It is an important part of Christianity that God is both transcendent and immanent.

How may God be known?

There are two main kinds of **revelation** in Christianity by which theists believe that God may be known: general revelation and special revelation.

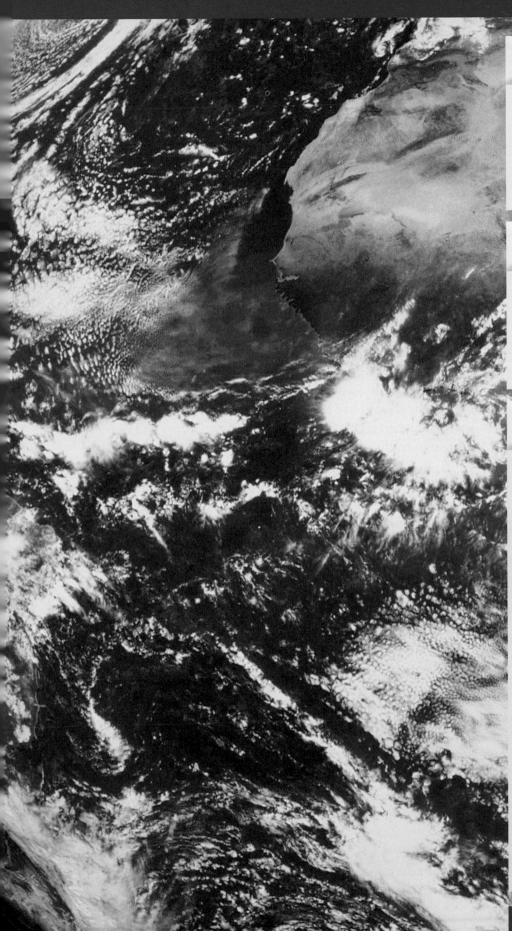

What is...?

Some theists refer to God as **personal**. They believe that God is a conscious individual or person with whom people are able to have a relationship or feel close to.

Some theists refer to God as **impersonal**. They believe that God has no 'human' side.

What is...?

A **revelation** is when something that was previously hidden becomes visible or something that was not known becomes clear. For a religious believer, this will be something about God or the way in which God wants people to behave.

Questions

1 Explain what is meant when a theist states God is 'immanent'.
2 Explain what is meant when a theist states God is 'transcendent'.
3 Do Christians believe God is immanent or transcendent? Give reasons for your answer.
4 What aspects or attributes of God does a Christian accept when they describe God as eternal, omniscient, omnipresent, and omnipotent?
5 What does a religious believer mean by a 'revelation'?
6 What does a Christian mean by 'general revelation'?
7 How might the beauty and power of nature act as a general revelation for a religious believer?
8 'An immanent God is better than a transcendent one.' Do you agree? Give reasons for your answer, showing that you have thought about more than one point of view.

General revelation

Activity

One form of general revelation is seeing the presence of God in nature. Look back at the Design argument on page 10 and religious experience found in nature on page 12. Write a paragraph to explain how the natural world might act as a general revelation.

What is...?

Vatican II was a Council of the Catholic Church. The Council met between 11 October 1962 and 8 December 1965. The Council met to reconsider Catholic doctrine (teaching) on many new issues facing the Church. On some issues, the Council re-emphasised the traditional teaching of the Church, but on others it led to many significant changes in the Catholic Church. Vatican II has been an important source of moral authority for Catholics.

General revelation

Religious traditions teach that God may be known through revelation. For Christians, general revelation is God making himself known through ordinary, common human experiences or natural means. General revelation is indirect and available to everyone. General revelation includes:

- seeing the presence of God in nature
- seeing God in writings of religious leaders
- seeing God in other people through their life and work
- seeing God's character revealed through reason, conscience and conviction.

Religious writings

The writings of religious leaders help other Christians understand the nature of God. Some religious leaders, past and present, write explanations of bible passages to help Christians understand what the Bible reveals about God, or they may publish reports on how Christians should live their lives according to the will of God. The importance given by Christians to these writings will depend on the Christian tradition to which they belong.

For example, the Pope is the Head of the Catholic Church. The Pope gives guidance to Catholics on matters of faith and morality through statements called encyclicals. A famous encyclical called *Humanae Vitae* ('On Human Life') was issued by Pope Paul VI in 1968. This encyclical stated the traditional Catholic teaching about the use of birth control and still influences the lives of Catholics today. *Humanae Vitae* was an important source of moral authority.

The General Synod of the Church of England was set up in 1970 so that everyone, bishops, clergy and laity, could share in governing the Church. It is the only group of people to whom Parliament has given power to pass Measures (resolutions) that become English law. The General Synod sets the rules and regulations of the Church and covers many areas of church life such as the difficult decisions about the ordination of women. In recent years, the General Synod has debated, for example, homelessness, the future of the

The beauty of a sunset makes some people become aware of God working in the world

BBC, the plight of street children in South America, and the effects of Sunday trading. Such debates are usually supported by well-researched reports available to anyone who is interested.

The Pope guides Catholics on matters of faith and morality

Seeing God in other people

The way someone has behaved in their life and work is sometimes so extraordinary that religious believers feel that God has guided them in some way. By studying the life and work of these individuals, Christians believe that they can find out more about God.

There are many examples of Christians who have inspired others to believe in God because of the way in which they have lived their lives. The life and work of these individuals is a strong indicator for others that God exists and how God wants them to behave. This is especially true when people have been willing to die for their beliefs.

Reason, conscience and conviction

Some Christians believe that our ability to reason tells us about God. A medieval Archbishop of Canterbury, St Anselm, argued that because we can define what we mean by the word 'God' then that is evidence in itself that God exists. Other Christians would argue that because we have a conscience (that is, we know what is right and wrong) and feel guilty when we have done wrong, it is evidence of the existence of God. For others, the desire to worship God is evidence in itself of God. They have certainty that God exists and what God is like and this conviction is all that they need. This conviction is often called faith.

Activity

Using the Internet and/or library, research the life and work of one of the following Christians. Explain how the life and work of the Christian you have researched might act as a general revelation for others.

● Martin Luther King Jr

● Maximilian Kolbe

● Mother Teresa

● Nicky Cruz

● St Paul.

Questions ?

1 How might the writings of religious leaders act as a general revelation for a religious believer?

2 (a) Outline the life and work of a Christian that might act as a general revelation for other Christians.

(b) Explain how the life and work of the individual you have outlined in (a) has guided other Christians.

3 How might reason, conscience and conviction act as a general revelation for a believer?

cial revelation

The sick are brought on pilgrimage to Lourdes in the hope of a miraculous cure

Special revelation occurs when God is believed to have spoken directly to an individual or a group of people. It is different from a general revelation because it is not a general everyday experience that is there for everyone to see and believe in. It is 'specially' for one person or a group of people.

Special revelation includes conversion, which occurs when an incident or experience is believed to be directly from God and causes the person to have a change of belief.

Dreams

Dreams are one way in which people believe that they have had a direct (special) revelation from God. An example is when Joseph discovered Mary, the mother of Jesus, was pregnant. Joseph knew that the child was not his and he considered breaking off the engagement. But he was told in a dream that Mary had done nothing wrong and the child that she was expecting was to be called 'Jesus, because he will save his people from their sins'.

Visions

Visions are another form of special revelation in which people see Jesus, the Virgin Mary or saints, or hear messages from God. An example of a Christian who received visions was St Bernadette. She saw visions of the Virgin Mary and was told that the waters of Lourdes had healing properties.

Miraculous healing

Miraculous healing is when a person recovers from a serious illness or handicap in a way that medical science cannot explain. An amazing, inexplicable recovery like this often convinces people that God has intervened. Many Christians say that there have been many cases of miraculous healing at Lourdes, for example.

Different perspectives on revelation

Worship

Worship may be classed as both special and general revelation according to whether it is believed that God has made himself known directly or indirectly to the believer. For example, when some Christians claim to feel the direct presence of God during an act of worship, this is special revelation. For others, people's desire to worship God is general revelation.

Activity

1 Look back at the conversion of St Paul on the road to Damascus on page 15.

2 Write a paragraph to explain:

(a) how the conversion of St Paul is an example of special revelation.

(b) how the conversion of St Paul led to a general revelation for Christians.

Activity

Using the Internet and/or library, research the life of St Bernadette and Lourdes as a place of pilgrimage.

1 Write a paragraph to outline the visions St Bernadette received.

2 Write a paragraph to explain why Lourdes has become a place of pilgrimage.

How God may be known

Different Christian traditions do have some different views on how God may be known. In the past, different Christian traditions started because of this crucial question. For example, the Protestant tradition originated because some believers developed different views from the Catholic Church. Most Protestants argue that people could have direct contact with God through Jesus. They disagreed with the Catholic view that the way to God is through priests and saints.

On rare occasions, God is believed to have communicated directly with a Pope. As a result of this communication, a pope has the authority to issue an *ex cathedra* statement. Catholics believe that an *ex cathedra* statement is free from any error because it has come directly from God.

Protestants might believe that God inspires their leader in their work and writing (general revelation), but not directly.

Sacred texts

The Holy Book (that is, sacred writings) of Christians is the Bible. Many Christians argue that the Bible is special revelation because it is one way in which God communicates directly with individuals. Other Christians argue that the Word of God in the Bible is available to everyone and is general revelation.

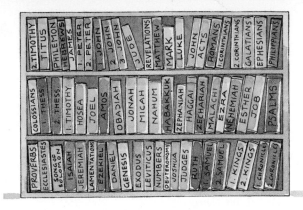

The Bible is not one book. It is a collection of 66 books, written over many centuries. As the Bible covers a long period of time, most Christians agree that the Bible reveals:

- how God has acted in the history of the world
- how God wants people to live their lives
- what God is like.

It is through studying the Bible that Christians believe it is revealed how God wants people to live their lives and what God is like. For example, the Ten Commandments and the teaching of Jesus are sources of moral authority.

Christians do not agree how God has 'spoken' through the Bible and how Bible passages are to be interpreted

Activity

Prayer, charismatic worship and sacramental worship are examples of special revelation. Look back at the sections 'Communicating with God through prayer and meditation', 'Charismatic worship' and 'Sacramental worship' on pages 12–13.

Write a paragraph to explain:

(a) how prayer is an example of special revelation.

(b) how charismatic worship is an example of special revelation.

(c) how sacramental worship is an example of special revelation.

Questions ?

1 How is special revelation different from general revelation?

2 How might worship be either general revelation or special revelation?

3 (a) Why do some Christians regard the Bible as special revelation?

   (b) Why do some Christians regard the Bible as general revelation?

4 'The Bible is the best way to know God.' Do you agree? Give reasons for your answer, showing that you have thought about more than one point of view.

Do you understand …

what people believe about the nature of God?

Task 1

Read the following statements and then answer the questions that follow.

> **A:** *'God is the creator.'*
>
> **B:** *'God is omnipotent.'*
>
> **C:** *'There are many gods.'*
>
> **D:** *'God is not a single being but a unity of beings.'*

1 **(a)** Which statement would be made by a polytheist?

  (b) Explain why you have chosen this statement for the polytheist.

  (c) What does a monotheist believe?

2 **(a)** Explain what Statement A means.

  (b) Outline a creation story found in **one** religious tradition.

3 Would religious believers agree with Statement D? Give reasons for your answer, showing that you have thought about more than one point of view.

4 **(a)** What does it mean to describe God as omnipotent?

  (b) State and explain **two** other attributes of God.

Task 2

1 **(a)** How is the belief in a personal God different from a belief in an impersonal God?

  (b) How is the belief in a transcendent God different from a belief in an immanent God?

2 Christians believe that God is in three parts, the Trinity.

  (a) Are Christians monotheists or polytheists? Explain your answer.

  (b) Explain which part(s) of the Trinity refer to a personal God and which part(s) refer to an impersonal God.

3 'It is better to worship many gods than just one God.' Do you agree? Give reasons for your answer, showing that you have thought about more than one point of view.

Task 3

1 Using examples from **two** religious traditions, explain what can be revealed about God through different religious writings.

2 What can a believer know about God through worship? Give examples to explain your answer.

3 Using examples from **two** religious traditions, explain what can be revealed about God through the lives and work of religious leaders.

4 'God can only be known through special revelation.' Do you agree? Give reasons for your answer, showing that you have thought about more than one point of view.

Task 4

Read the following passages and answer the questions that follow.

Christians agree that God inspired the Bible and it is one way by which God has made himself known to the world; but Christians do not agree how God has 'spoken' through the Bible and how bible passages are to be interpreted, that is, explained so as to make the meaning clear. This is why, for some Christians, the Bible is a special revelation and for others it is a general revelation.

Fundamentalist Christians believe the Bible is the direct Word of God, dictated to the writers as if by a heavenly voice, and therefore everything in the Bible is the literal truth. The writers had direct contact with God so the writers received special revelation. Since the Bible states that the world was created in six days, Fundamentalists believe in a six-day creation. Fundamentalists argue that if the Bible appears to contradict science then it is science that is wrong. As the Bible is the Word of God then there are no errors in the Bible as God has guided the writers and it is the only revelation needed.

Progressive Christians believe that the writers of the Bible did not record God's message word for word but brought their personalities and writing styles to each event. These Christians believe that the Bible is the Word of God interpreted. For example, they would say that the Bible does not give an exact account of creation, but is a guide to help humans understand God's role in creation. It is a book about faith and knowledge of God; it is not intended to be a scientific textbook. These Christians believe the Bible contains truths inspired by God and is general revelation.

Liberal Christians believe people who felt they had a special understanding of God's message wrote the Bible. Liberal Christians believe that the writers of the Bible were concerned with the people and events of their time and modern readers need to re-interpret its ideas in the light of modern understanding of the world to reveal aspects of God. This means that there are some things in the Bible that may not be relevant to our time and some things that may be wrong.

1 Look back at the Genesis account of creation on page 9.

2 Explain how a Fundamentalist, a Progressive and a Liberal Christian would interpret the Genesis account of creation.

3 Explain what a Fundamentalist, a Progressive and a Liberal Christian would understand about the nature of God from the Genesis account of creation.

4 What would be the different understandings about the Bible as a revelation from God of a Fundamentalist, a Progressive and a Liberal Christian?

Task 5

Read the following passages from the Bible and write an explanation of what may be learnt about the nature of God from these passages.

In the beginning, when God created the universe. (Genesis 1:1)

God is Spirit, and only by the power of his Spirit can people worship him as he really is. (John 4:24)

Ever since God created the world, his invisible qualities, both his eternal power and his divine nature, have been clearly seen; they are perceived in the things that God has made. (Romans 1:20)

God … knows everything. (1 John 3:20)

Task 6

Explain how the work of Christians seeking to help people with disabilities might be regarded as:

(a) general revelation

(b) special revelation.

Citizenship Link

1 Using the Internet and/or library, research some of the problems or challenges resulting from one of the following disabilities:

- total blindness
- profound deafness
- Down's syndrome
- hemophilia.

2 Design a leaflet for use by a religious organisation that helps people with the disability you have chosen. In your leaflet:

- explain the problems caused for the person with the disability
- ways in which others could help to relieve the suffering caused by the disability.

Morality

Read the following passage and answer the questions that follow.

A woman is diagnosed with cancer and she and her husband are told that she will only live for a few more months. The doctor tells them that there is a new treatment that would cure her cancer but it is only available in certain health authorities and, unfortunately, their authority is not one of them. The man asks: if he moved his wife to one of these health authorities, would she get the treatment? The doctor answers that they would have to be resident in the area for at least six months before she would be treated and she is unlikely to live that long. The man writes to the drug company and asks the cost of the drug. The man gave up his job to look after his wife so has a low income and cannot afford the cost quoted by the drug company. The man realises that the company is not far from where he lives and decides to break into the company and steal enough of the drug to cure his wife.

- The man has made a moral decision. List all the things that will have guided him in making this moral decision.

- Do you agree with his decision? Give reasons for your answer, showing that you have thought about different points of view.

- Discuss your view with your teacher and the rest of the class.

John Stuart Mill (1806–73)

Religious believers have tried to solve the problem of knowing how to behave in a moral way. They have developed different ethical theories to help people make moral decisions and to provide them with a framework for dealing with moral questions.

For some religious believers, it is the consequences of an action that needs to be considered to decide whether or not the action is moral. For example, in the case of the woman with cancer (see Activity), would stealing the drugs be morally right if the woman was cured?

Other religious believers look at the motives of an action to decide whether or not the action is moral. For example, in the case of the woman with cancer (see Activity), has the man made the decision to steal the drugs because he loves his wife and wants to relieve her suffering?

Utilitarianism

Jeremy Bentham (1748–1832) and John Stuart Mill (1806–73) were two philosophers who developed the moral philosophy of utilitarianism. According to their theory, the consequences of an action should be considered, rather than its motives. If the consequences of the action result in the greatest happiness for the greatest number of people then the action is morally right. 'Rule utilitarianism' and 'Act utilitarianism' are two forms of this philosophy

Rule utilitarians judge the morality of an action according to the consequences of everybody breaking the rule. Rule utilitarians believe there is far greater happiness for the majority in a society if everyone keeps a particular rule. It would be morally wrong to break a rule if that rule is for the benefit of society as a whole. Therefore, everyone, regardless of the situation, must keep all rules. This is an example of **absolute morality**.

Act utilitarians judge the morality of an action according to the consequences of that individual situation. In each individual situation, the action that results in the greatest happiness for the greatest number is the action that an Act utilitarian would judge to be morally right in that specific situation. The rule is applied to each individual situation and there may be times when better consequences are achieved by ignoring the rule. This is an example of **relative morality**.

Situation ethics

Situation **ethics** is a theory developed by Joseph Fletcher in the 1960s. It attempts to develop a guide to how to behave in the right way, which could be applied to each situation or circumstance. Fletcher said that an action is morally right if the intention (motive) is to show Christian love (**agape**). The consequences of an action might not turn out as intended, but if the motive behind the action was love then it is a morally right act. Fletcher suggests that certain acts, such as lying and theft, may be morally right, depending on the situation. Situation ethics is an example of relative morality.

What do you think?

The man stole the drugs and was caught and sent to prison for his offence. His wife never received the drugs and died while he was in prison. In a small group or with your teacher, discuss the following questions.

- Did the man behave in a moral way?
- Was it right that he was sent to prison when all he wanted to do was cure his wife?
- Would a utilitarian have agreed with his action?
- Would a supporter of situation ethics believe that he had shown Christian love?

What is...?

Morality is conduct based on the distinction between right and wrong.

Ethics is the study of how people behave as regards right and wrong conduct. Ethics is the study of morality.

What is...?

Absolute morality sees what is morally right and wrong as fixed, applying to all circumstances at all times.

Relative morality sees what is morally right and wrong as varying, depending on individual circumstances.

Agape is Christian love. Jesus taught that love of God includes loving your neighbour as yourself. He said that people must act out of unconditional love in every action they take. Christians try to follow this teaching. If someone who needs help is ignored then they believe that God is ignored.

Activity

1 Look again at the incident of the man who stole the drugs.

2 In small groups or with your teacher, work out how a Rule utilitarian and an Act utilitarian would answer the statement that 'The man should not have gone to prison for his theft.'

Sources of moral authority 2

Christians try to live according to the teaching of Jesus

Religious leaders

The head of a whole religious tradition, such as the Pope as head of the Catholic Church, can be a source of moral authority for all Christians within that tradition. Or the leader of their local community may guide some Christians on how to behave. For example, a minister or priest may give a talk (sermon) in the services to remind the congregation of how God expects them to behave.

Culture and upbringing

How people are brought up will influence what an individual considers to be right or wrong behaviour. If people are taught from an early age that certain types of behaviour are wrong then it is likely that those views will stay with them for life. The culture of your society will also influence your moral attitudes. If society condemns certain types of behaviour then people are likely to avoid committing those sorts of acts.

Reason

Christians will think a problem or situation through in their own mind. They will reason out the best course of action. Christians will use other sources of moral authority such as the Bible to help them to reason through the situation and decide the moral course to take.

Conscience

Conscience is used to describe a person's own sense of right and wrong and feelings of guilt when a person thinks that they have done something wrong. The final guide for most Christians as to whether they have come to the right moral decision is their conscience.

For many Christians, conscience is regarded as the inner voice of God that is telling them how to behave. Christians who accept conscience as a guide from God believe that it they feel ashamed or frightened, or that they are doing wrong then God is telling them that the action is wrong. For many Christians, this belief that God is speaking to them through their conscience is further evidence of the existence of God.

Values

Values are what people consider important or desirable as a guide to living a moral life. For a Christian, these values reflect the central beliefs of the Christian faith. However, the response of one Christian to an ethical issue may be very different from that of another Christian. This is because Christians do not always agree on how the sources of moral authority should be interpreted.

For example, if Christians try to live their lives according to Jesus' command to 'love their neighbour', they may do this in different ways. Some Christians believe their role is to pray for those in need or to raise money to give practical aid. Other Christians believe that they must take an active role in improving the lives of those less fortunate than themselves in some way. Situation ethics is one moral philosophy that some Christians use to show 'love of their neighbour', whereas other Christians may believe that Liberation theology is a better way.

Liberation theology

Liberation theology is a moral philosophy that teaches that Christians must help to free people from injustice. Liberation theology teaches that Christians must not only help to save people's souls but also help them to achieve freedom from oppression and exploitation.

Liberation theology is popular in Latin American countries. In these countries, 90 per cent of the people live in poverty and struggle every day to have enough money on which to live. The aim of Liberationists is to change the lives of the poor so that they can achieve a better quality of life. This means that these societies will have to change. If the poor are to have a better standard of living then the rich will have to give up some of their wealth.

Activity

1 Look back at the roles of Christian religious leaders on page 36.

2 Explain the ways in which the leaders in different Christian traditions act as sources of moral authority.

Questions ?

1 How did Jesus summarise the Ten Commandments?

2 How might a person's upbringing influence their moral code?

3 What is meant by 'conscience'?

4 'It is easier to be told what to do than to have to work it out for yourself.' Do you agree? Give reasons for your answer, showing that you have thought about more than one point of view.

Do you understand ...

about ways of making moral decisions?

Task 1

1 Find an article in one of today's newspapers that you believe involves making decisions about right and wrong.
2 Explain why you believe there is a moral decision to be made.
3 Explain what would influence a Christian in making this moral decision.
4 Explain the distinction between a Christian who takes an absolute moral stance from a Christian who takes a relative moral stance.

Task 2

1 Explain what a Christian means by 'agape'.
2 How does the teaching of Jesus support agape?
3 Explain how a Christian might show agape.

Task 3

Explain how each of the following help Christians to make moral decisions.

- The teaching found in the Bible
- Teachings from the Christian traditions
- Religious leaders
- Culture and upbringing
- Reason
- Conscience.

Task 4

1 Why do some people believe that religion and morality are related to each other?
2 Why do you think that people believe that if everybody kept the last five of the Ten Commandments we would live in a more moral society?

3 If you were able to add an eleventh commandment what would it be? Give reasons for your choice.

Task 5

Explain what determines whether an action is morally right or wrong for a Christian who accepts:

(a) situation ethics

(b) utilitarianism.

Jeremy Bentham (1748–1832) was the founder of utilitarianism

Task 6

Oscar Romero became Archbishop of San Salvador in 1977. At that time there was growing unrest in the country as the majority of the population lived in poverty. Christians began to form groups for study, worship and discussion, aiming to follow the Gospels and their teachings for society. These groups had their own priest and an elected leader from the group. The ruling class were frightened that the uneducated peasants were concerning themselves with social issues in the name of Christianity. Many of these Christians were persecuted and some died under 'mysterious circumstances'.

Archbishop Romero spoke out against the injustices in the country. Romero said: 'I am bound, as a pastor, by divine command to give my life for those whom I love, and that is all Salvadorians, even those who are going to kill me.' Two weeks later he was assassinated while celebrating Holy Communion.

1 Why do you think that Archbishop Romero believed that as a Christian he had a duty to fight injustice?

2 What do you think Archbishop Romero meant when he said: 'I am bound, as a pastor, by divine command to give my life for those whom I love'?

3 In what ways might Archbishop Romero act as a source of moral authority for other Christians?

Oscar Romero (1917–80)

Citizenship Link

Organise a class debate to consider the following statement: 'Religious believers should not be involved in politics.' In the speech you write for the debate, think about:

- the different sources of authority religious believers use to make moral decisions

- the influences that religious views might have on the moral life of the country

- why religious believers might wish to be involved in politics.

Sanctity and quality of life

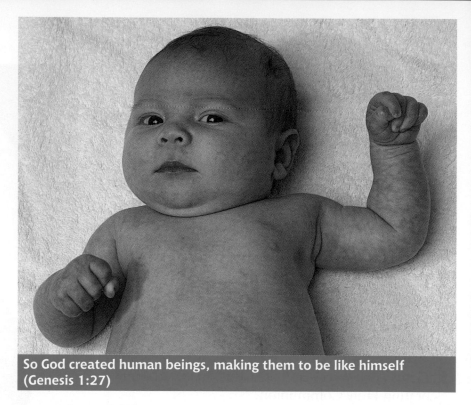

So God created human beings, making them to be like himself (Genesis 1:27)

What is...?

Sanctity of life is the view that life is sacred because God gave life and human beings should not end it.

Activity

1 Read the biblical extracts below.

2 Write a paragraph to explain why these passages might lead a Christian to believe that life is sacred.

   Do not commit murder. (Exodus 20:13)

   Surely you know that you are God's temple and that God's spirit lives in you! So if anyone destroys God's temple, God will destroy him. For God's temple is holy, and you yourselves are his temple. (1 Corinthians 3:16–17)

Sanctity of life

Issues such as abortion are linked to the Christian belief in the **sanctity of life**. When Christians state that life has sanctity, they are saying that life is special to God. Each person is a separate, living human being with rights, especially the right to life. Christian beliefs about God as creator include the belief that all human beings are created as individuals. Every individual is unique and unlike any other individual in the universe. Human beings have a special place in God's eyes and in God's creation.

Most Christians believe that God is the Lord of life because he is the creator, and because God has given life to everyone, it is only right that he decides when it begins and ends. As life comes from God then the belief has developed that life itself is sacred – it is holy and set apart for God. This means that life must be protected and used in the way in which God would want.

The book of Genesis in the Bible describes God's creation of the universe. The Bible explains that God's creation of man and woman was personal. Human beings were made in the image, or likeness, of God.

Christians do not agree on how the phrase 'in our image, in our likeness' is to be understood. For some Christians it means that in some way they physically resemble God, but for other Christians it means God has given them some control over their own life, that is, the right to make their own decisions. So for some Christians, ending a human life is wrong because it would be ending a life in which there is a part of God. For other Christians, ending a human life in certain circumstances is acceptable, as God has allowed each individual the free will to make their own decisions.

Quality of life

When making moral decisions related to issues such as abortion, some Christians consider not only the sanctity of life but also the quality of life. When Christians judge the quality of life, they do not consider how rich a person is or how many possessions they have. Quality of life is about an individual's awareness of self and the world in which he or she lives, and the ability to get something more than pain and suffering out of life.

Can one person judge the quality of life of another?

Stephen Hawking (pictured) suffers from motor neuron disease. The result is that he is confined to a wheelchair and has to communicate via a computer. This is a quality of life with which many people would feel that they could not cope. Yet despite his disabilities, Stephen Hawking remains one of the leading physicists of the day and has written many best-selling books. This raises the question in many people's minds as to whether it is ever possible for one person to make a decision regarding the quality of another person's life. Some Christians would argue that only God could make such a decision.

Questions ?

1 Explain the term 'sanctity of life', supporting your answer with religious teaching.
2 Explain the term 'quality of life'.
3 The Genesis account of creation teaches Christians that they are made in the 'image' and 'likeness' of God. Explain how different Christians might understand this concept.

The right to abortion

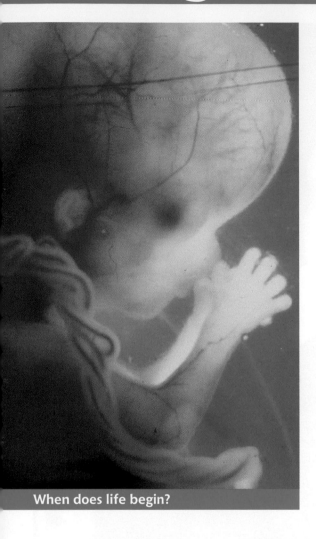

When does life begin?

The law on abortion

In 1967 Parliament passed an Abortion Act, which made **abortion** legal if it was performed in the first 28 weeks of the pregnancy. The Human Fertilisation and Embryology Act 1990 reduced the time in which a legal termination is permitted to twenty-four weeks. An abortion is legal if two doctors agree that one of the following circumstances exists:

1 there is risk to the life of the mother if the pregnancy continued, or

2 there is risk of injury to the mental or physical health of the mother, or

3 there is a substantial risk that, if the child were born, it would suffer from physical or mental abnormalities, or

4 there is risk to the physical or mental well being of her existing children if the pregnancy continues.

Although no Christian traditions encourage abortion, they are not in agreement as to whether or not abortion should ever be allowed. Some Protestants believe that in certain circumstances abortion may be the lesser of two evils and would support the right to abortion. On the other hand, the Catholic Church would argue that an abortion is always a sin.

The Bible has no direct teaching related to abortion and in making the moral decision as to whether or not to allow an abortion, Christians will also use other sources of moral authority (see pages 36–7). As part of the decision-making process, Christians have to consider the importance of the 'sanctity of life' and 'quality of life' and decide when they believe life begins.

The Catholic Church opposes abortion. Some Catholics are members of pro-life organisations such as Save the Unborn Child that campaigns against abortion. Protestant Churches such as the Church of England and Methodists support the right to abortion in certain circumstances. Some Protestants support a woman's right to choose, and work for organisations such as The Abortion Reform Group or Christians for Free Choice.

Arguments supporting abortion

Some Protestants who support the right to abortion believe that it is an evil to be avoided if at all possible. However, they do agree that abortion could be justifiable if it meant that greater evils were avoided. Other Protestants do not see abortion as an evil, but simply part of a woman's right to choose. The circumstances under which some Christians support abortion include the following.

- Abortion has been made legal under UK law and is not murder as it destroys only a collection of cells. Therefore, legal abortion is not breaking the sixth commandment, 'Do not commit murder.'

- Abortion could be justified if there were a risk to the physical or mental health of the mother (Church of England Resolution 1983), if she were likely to give birth to a child with serious physical or mental abnormalities, or if the pregnancy were the result of incest or rape.

- The decision to continue a pregnancy should not be forced on a woman but left to her own conscience. The Church of England stresses that the feelings and the wishes of the mother have to be respected (Church of England Resolution 1974).

- The Methodist Church argues that if the family is in economic difficulties and another baby would add to the financial burden on the family and cause further deprivation to the existing children then an abortion should be allowed.

- Jesus taught Christians to 'love their neighbour' and some Christians argue that an abortion may be the most loving action. Their view is that it is wrong to bring unwanted children into the world, especially if a child is seriously handicapped. It may be better that the potential life is returned to God and support their argument with the words of Jesus when he said, 'Let the children come to me and do not stop them, because the Kingdom of God belongs to such as these' (Luke 18:16).

- Before abortions were made legal, many women went to 'back street' abortionists. These were illegal abortions, often performed by untrained people in unhygienic conditions. As a result, many women were seriously injured and about 30 women died each year. If it becomes more difficult to get legalised abortions, there would be a return to illegal 'back street' abortions.

- Quakers (The Society of Friends) have not issued a corporate statement on abortion. A central Quaker belief is that there is 'that of God in everyone' and so are opposed to the taking of human life. However, as with many other Christian traditions, Quakers are undecided when human life begins. Some Quakers oppose abortion because they believe God is in the foetus from conception, but there are other Quakers who think that in some circumstances, abortion may be the only alternative. Many Quakers believe that God guides people through their conscience and if an abortion is felt to be the right course of action then other Quakers must respect that decision.

Activity

1. Look back at page 36–7.

2. Give **two** sources of moral authority that Christians might use to support a woman's right to abortion.

3. Is the argument for the right to abortion under certain circumstances an example of absolute morality or relative morality?

Arguments against abortion

The Catholic Church teaches that life is a gift from God that may only be ended by God. Catholics are taught that life begins at the moment of conception and abortion is therefore murder. Abortion breaks the sixth commandment from God not to kill. This teaching is set out in the Catechism of the Catholic Church, where it says that:

> *Human life must be respected and protected absolutely from the moment of conception. From the first moment of its existence, a human being must be recognised as having the rights of a person – among which is the inviolable right of every innocent being to life.*

The leaders of the Catholic Church teach that abortion is a sin. In 1968, in the encyclical *Humanae Vitae* ('On Human Life'), Pope Paul VI stated that it is an absolute rule for all Catholics that abortion was wrong. The only exception to this is when abortion happens as an inevitable result of medical treatment the mother has to have. The Second Vatican Council described abortion as 'an abominable crime'.

The Catholic tradition supports the teaching that abortion is wrong with biblical passages. Here are some key passages and their interpretations.

Psalm 127:3 states that 'Children are a gift from the Lord; they are a real blessing'. Some Christians would argue that it is not necessary to have an abortion because if the mother does not want the child or cannot cope, there are many childless couples who would welcome the chance to adopt a child so there is never an unwanted baby.

Many childless couples would welcome the chance to adopt an unwanted baby

Many biblical passages teach that every life is unique and planned by God. Catholics teach that God knows who we are before we are conceived so an abortion would be going against God's plan. We can never know how valuable a life is going to be. For example, the prophet Isaiah wrote that 'Before I was born, the Lord appointed me; he made me his servant' (Isaiah 49:5). St Paul wrote that God had chosen him as his servant before he was born: 'But God in his grace chose me even before I was born, and called me to serve him' (Galatians 1:15).

In Acts 17:26 it states that God has decided when we will live and for how long. Life is a gift from God that may only be ended by God: 'He himself fixed beforehand the exact times and the limits of the places where they would live.'

Jesus did not speak specifically about abortion, but Catholics believe that it is possible to look at his teaching and his actions and conclude that he would oppose it. Jesus helped the sick and disabled as well as those who were unwanted, and people must seek to do the same. Catholics believe that he would want handicapped children helped, not their lives ended by abortion. Jesus said: 'See that you don't despise any of these little ones' (Matthew 18:10) and 'whoever welcomes in my name one such child as this, welcomes me' (Matthew 18:5). Some Christians would argue that people do not have the right to make decisions about what the quality of life of an unborn child would be.

Jesus taught that people should share their wealth so there would be no need for women to seek abortions if there was sufficient provisions to help them overcome any emotional and financial difficulties the pregnancy would cause. (Look at Jesus' teaching about the use of wealth on pages 150–1.)

Luke 1:44 says that from the moment of conception, the unborn child is aware of its identity and the world. The unborn baby might feel the pain of the abortion. When the Virgin Mary visited her cousin Elizabeth, Elizabeth, who was pregnant with John the Baptist, said that the baby knew that the child within Mary's womb was special: 'For as soon as I heard your greeting, the baby within me jumped with gladness.'

Most Christians, including Catholics, accept that there may be emergency medical procedures that have to be performed to save the life of the mother that also inevitably ends the pregnancy. This is because of the double effect rule. The doctors are seeking to save the life of the mother, not to terminate the pregnancy, so the medical procedure is morally acceptable.

Activity

1 Look back at the sources of moral authority that Christians use to help them to make moral decisions on pages 36–7.

2 Give **two** sources of moral authority that Christians might use to oppose abortion.

3 Are the arguments against abortion examples of absolute morality or relative morality?

Questions ?

1 What is an abortion?
2 Explain in your own words the current abortion law of England and Wales.
3 'The Bible commands, "Do not kill". Therefore, abortion is clearly wrong.' Do you agree? Give reasons for your answer, showing that you have thought about more than one point of view. Refer to religious teachings in your answer.

Do you understand ...

about the issues surrounding abortion?

Task 1

You created every part of me; you put me together in my mother's womb ... When my bones were formed, carefully put together in my mother's womb, when I was growing there in secret, you knew that I was there – you saw me before I was born. (Psalm 139:13, 15)

1 Explain the terms 'sanctity of life' and 'quality of life'.

2 How might Christians apply the extract from Psalm 139:13, 15 to these two ideas?

3 How might Christians apply the idea of the sanctity of life to the moral issue of abortion?

Task 2

Look at the pictures below and answer the questions that follow.

1 What view about legalised abortion do you think people in picture A will take? Give reasons for your answer.

2 What view about legalised abortion do you think people in picture B will take? Give reasons for your answer.

3 Explain which view you agree with, including reasons for your view.

Task 3

A pregnant woman has been told that the baby she is carrying will be born severely handicapped.

1 Explain why believers of **one** religious tradition are against abortion in the situation above. Support your answer with religious teaching.

2 Explain why believers in a different religious tradition think that abortion may be justified in the situation above. Support your answer with religious teaching.

3 State and explain **two** circumstances, other than the example above, when abortion is regarded by some Christians as acceptable.

4 'If a baby is not wanted by its mother, there are many people who would adopt it. It should not be murdered.' Do you agree? Give reasons for your answer, showing that you have thought about more than one point of view. Refer to religious teachings in your answer.

Picture B

Picture A

46

Task 4

Read the passage below and answer the questions that follow.

In 1995, Pope John Paul II declared that the Church's teaching on abortion:

is unchanged and unchangeable. Therefore, by the authority, which Christ conferred upon Peter and his successors, I declare that direct abortion, that is, abortion willed as an end or as a means, always constitutes a grave moral disorder, since it is the deliberate killing of an innocent human being. This doctrine is based upon the natural law and upon the written Word of God, is transmitted by the Church's tradition and taught by the ordinary and universal magisterium [leading authorities]. *No circumstance, no purpose, no law whatsoever can ever make licit* [right, lawful] *an act which is intrinsically illicit* [wrong, unlawful], *since it is contrary to the law of God which is written in every human heart, knowable by reason itself, and proclaimed by the Church.'* (Evangelium Vitae 62, 'Gospel of Life')

Pope John Paul II

1 *Evangelium Vitae* was a declaration made by Pope John Paul II about abortion. How would Catholics use this declaration as a source of moral authority?

2 Why does Pope John Paul II oppose any abortions?

3 Is this declaration an example of relative or absolute morality? Give reasons for your answer.

4 Why might some Christian traditions not agree with Pope John Paul II's declaration?

Task 5

Read the following passage and answer the questions that follow.

A Church of England Resolution in 1983 stated: 'All human life, including life developing in the womb, is created by God in his own image and is, therefore, to be nurtured, supported and protected,' but added in a later resolution in 1984, 'The life of a foetus is not absolutely sacrosanct if it endangers the life of the mother.' This is because the Church of England believes 'that abortion is an evil, but that to withhold compassion is evil. Christians need to face frankly that in an imperfect world the "right" choice is sometimes the acceptance of the lesser of two evils.'

1 How would members of the Church of England use these resolutions as a source of moral authority?

2 What is the teaching of the Church of England about abortion?

3 Are these resolutions an example of relative or absolute morality? Give reasons for your answer.

Citizenship Link

Prepare a speech for a class debate on the following statement: 'The abortion law should be changed to only allow legal abortions in the first twelve weeks of the pregnancy.' Your speech can support or oppose the motion.

Sex before marriage

He bought you for a price

Most Christians believe that the Bible makes it clear that God does not want people who are not married to each other to have sex together. This includes sex before marriage (**pre-marital sex**) as well as **extra-marital sex (adultery)**.

The early Christian leader, St Paul, taught that the best way to serve God was to be **celibate**, but if people could not control their sexual desires then they must marry to avoid sin.

> *Now, to deal with the matters you wrote about.*

> *A man does well not to marry. But because there is so much immorality, every man should have his own wife, and every woman should have her own husband.*
> *(1 Corinthians 7:1–2)*

> *Now, to the unmarried and to the widows I say that it would be better for you to continue to live alone as I do. But if you cannot restrain your desires, go ahead and marry – it is better to marry than to burn with passion.*
> *(1 Corinthians 7: 8–9)*

St Paul said that the body should be kept pure as a 'temple to the Holy Spirit', and sex outside marriage is a sin that makes the body spiritually unclean.

> *Avoid immorality. Any other sin a man commits does not affect his body; but the man who is guilty of sexual immorality sins against his own body. Don't you know that your body is the temple of the Holy Spirit, who lives in you and who was given to you by God? You do not belong to yourselves but to God; he bought you for a price. So use your bodies for God's glory.*
> *(1 Corinthians 6:18–20)*

The Old Testament stresses the importance of virginity. A woman was expected to be a virgin on her wedding day and if it was found that she was not then she could be stoned to death.

What is...?

Celibacy is not having sexual relationships.

Chastity is to keep oneself sexually pure.

Pre-marital sex is sexual intercourse between two people who are not married.

Extra-marital sex is sexual intercourse between a couple when at least one of them is already married to another person. The other name used for extra-marital intercourse is **adultery**.

Laws concerning sexual purity (Deuteronomy 22:13–21)

'Suppose a man marries a woman and later he decides he doesn't want her. So he makes up false charges against her, accusing her of not being a virgin when they got married.

'If this happens, the woman's parents are to take the blood-stained wedding sheet that proves she was a virgin, and they are to show it in court to the town leaders. Her father will say to them, "I gave my daughter to this man in marriage, and now he doesn't want her. He has made false charges against her, saying that she was not a virgin when he married her. But here is the proof that my daughter was a virgin; look at the bloodstains on the wedding sheet!" Then the town leaders are to take the husband and beat him. They are also to fine him a hundred pieces of silver and give the money to the woman's father, because the man has brought disgrace on an Israelite woman. Moreover, she will continue to be his wife, and he can never divorce her as long as he lives.

'But if the charge is true and there is no proof that she was a virgin, then they are to take her out to the entrance of her father's house, where the men of her city are to stone her to death. She has done a shameful thing among our people by having intercourse before she was married, while she was still living in her father's house. In this way you will get rid of this evil.'

No one would be likely to say that Old Testament teaching on punishing pre-marital sex should be followed today in the UK. Our society is very different from Old Testament society. But some Christians would argue that people should understand the serious consequences pre-marital sex can bring: unwanted pregnancies and an increase in sexually transmitted diseases. They might say that if biblical teaching were obeyed, there would not be these current problems in society. Most Christians condemn casual sex as it is not within a lasting relationship and degrades what is regarded as a gift from God.

Activity

1 Write a summary of St Paul's teaching about sex outside marriage.

2 What do you think St Paul meant when he said, 'You do not belong to yourselves but to God; he bought you for a price'?

What do you think? ?

Few modern Western brides are virgins on their wedding day. Do you think that it is wrong for a bride who is not a virgin to wear a white dress? Give reasons for your answer.

The white wedding dress was regarded as a symbol of the bride's virginity

Questions ?

1 Why do you think that it was important in the past for a bride to be a virgin on her wedding day?

2 Why have attitudes to virginity changed in modern society?

3 'Some Christians believe people should wait until they are married before they have sex.' Do you agree? Give reasons for your answer, showing that you have thought about more than one point of view. Refer to religious teaching in your answer.

Sex outside marriage

Some Christian traditions, including the Catholic Church, teach that sex should only be between married couples and do not approve of any form of sexual activity outside marriage. However, other traditions do not agree. The Quakers accept that many people do not live in married relationships. The Church of England teaches that sex within marriage is the ideal but recognises that in modern society many couples have sex outside of marriage. The Church of England no longer refers to unmarried couples as 'living in sin' and accepts that sex between two people in a permanent relationship is an expression of love.

Same-sex relationships

Because same-sex marriages are not legal in the UK, all same-sex relationships exist outside marriage. Christian traditions are divided about same-sex relationships. The Quakers do not see homosexuality as a sin. The Catholic Church teaches that homosexual acts are unnatural and must be avoided. They believe that St Paul's teaching in his letter to the Romans supports this view:

> *Because they do this, God has given them over to shameful passions. Even the women pervert the natural use of their sex by unnatural acts. In the same way the men give up natural sexual relations with women and burn with passion for each other, and as a result they bring upon themselves the punishment they deserve for their wrongdoing. (Romans 1:26–7)*

What is...?

Lust means to have a physical desire for someone.

Activity

1 Read the incident of the woman caught in adultery in John 8:2–11.

2 Outline the incident in your own words.

3 Write a paragraph to explain what you think that this incident teaches a Christian who discovers that his or her marriage partner has been unfaithful.

The punishment for a woman who committed adultery at the time of Jesus was to be stoned to death

Teaching about adultery and divorce (Matthew 5:27–32)

You have heard that it was said, 'Do not commit adultery.' But now I tell you: anyone who looks at a woman and wants to possess her is guilty of committing adultery with her in his heart. So if your right eye causes you to sin, take it out and throw it away! It is much better for you to lose a part of your body than to have your whole body thrown into hell. If your right hand causes you to sin, cut it off and throw it away! It is much better for you to lose one of your limbs than for your whole body to go to hell.

It was also said, 'Anyone who divorces his wife must give her a written notice of divorce.' But now I tell you: if a man divorces his wife, for any cause other than her unfaithfulness, then he is guilty of making her commit adultery if she marries again; and the man who marries her commits adultery also.

The Church of England agrees that homosexual acts are not what God intended. However, many members of the Anglican Church will accept same-sex relationships if they are within a loving relationship, and some vicars have performed a 'marriage' ceremony to bless the relationship. Other members of the Church of England share the Catholic view that homosexuality is a sin.

Adultery

Another form of sexual relationship that most Christians condemn is adultery. The seventh commandment states that people must not commit adultery and the tenth that people must not desire other people's marriage partner. Jesus taught that not only is adultery wrong but also to look at someone 'lustfully'.

Jesus is warning that lustful thoughts are the motive behind adultery. He is trying to stop people from following a course of action that could lead to sin. When he refers to gouging out an eye, he is meaning that people have to take steps that are painful to stop something worse happening to them. He means it may be difficult to avoid giving in to the temptation to have an affair, but it is better to do that than to end up being punished by God. Hell will be a far worse fate.

Questions ?

1 Explain the attitude of **two** Christian traditions to sex outside marriage.
2 Explain why Jesus thought lustful thoughts were equal to adultery.
3 The suggestion that one should gouge out an eye or cut off a hand sounds extreme. Explain what Jesus was trying to teach when he gave these instructions.
4 'Sex outside marriage is a sin.' Do you agree? Give reasons for your answer, showing that you have thought about more than one point of view. Refer to religious teaching in your answer.

Sex within marriage

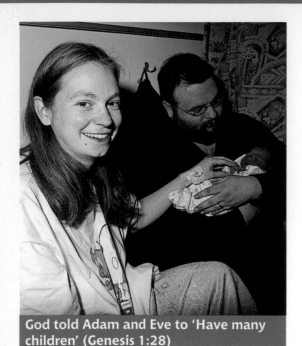

God told Adam and Eve to 'Have many children' (Genesis 1:28)

Jesus and St Paul taught that marriage is for life and adultery is a sin. When a couple marry and have sexual intercourse they become 'one flesh'. Only God may end this bond when one of the partners dies. The result is that the Christian marriage ceremonies include the vow to be faithful for life.

St Paul taught that sex within marriage was a gift from God and within the framework of marriage is not a sin. Husbands and wives should 'fulfil' their 'marital duty' to each other. He meant that there should be sexual intercourse between them so that neither partner is tempted to commit adultery. If they decided to refrain from sexual relations, for example, to devote themselves to prayer, then it must be by 'mutual consent' and for a limited time.

> *A man should fulfil his duty as a husband, and a woman should fulfil her duty as a wife, and each should satisfy the other's needs. A wife is not the master of her own body, but her husband is; in the same way a husband is not the master of his own body, but his wife is. Do not deny yourselves to each other, unless you first agree to do so for a while in order to spend your time in prayer; but then resume normal marital relations. In this way you will be kept from giving in to Satan's temptation because of your lack of self-control. (1 Corinthians 7:3–7)*

There is no direct teaching related to the use of contraception in the Bible, but some Christians have interpreted God's instruction to Adam and Eve to 'be fruitful and increase in number' to mean that the main purpose of sexual intercourse is to reproduce. This has led Christians to question the use of contraception.

Some Christian traditions, including the Catholic Church, teach that the purpose of sexual intercourse is to produce children and condemns the use of artificial methods of contraception as a sin. In *Humanae Vitae*, ('Of Human Life'), Pope Paul VI allowed the use of natural forms of contraception (the rhythm method):

> *The Church teaches that married people may then take advantage of the natural cycle immanent in the reproductive system and engage in marital intercourse only during those*

What is...?

An **arranged marriage** is a marriage in which the parents have found the marriage partner for their child.

Activity

1 Using the Internet and/or the library, find out more about the practice of arranged marriages in Islam, Hinduism and Sikhism.

2 Write a short explanation of why some religious traditions believe that it is the best way to find a marriage partner.

What do you think? ?

What do you think St Paul meant when he said that it was better that a couple resume normal marital relations so they will 'be kept from giving in to Satan's temptation because of your lack of self-control'?

times that are infertile, thus controlling birth in a way which does not in the least offend the moral principles.

But he condemned artificial methods. Although the Catholic Church condemns the use of artificial methods of contraception, many English Catholics do use such methods, as they believe that their conscience tells them that God does not disapprove.

The Church of England does not condemn the use of any form of contraception. It was the first church to allow contraception under certain circumstances (in 1930). The other Protestant Churches then followed. These Churches teach the importance of 'planned parenthood' and allow a couple to take precautions until they feel ready to become parents.

Choice of a marriage partner

In some religions, the choice of marriage partner is considered too important to be left to the individual alone. The parents have greater experience of life and know the character of their child so their choice of marriage partner will be a wise one. In Hinduism, Islam and Sikhism, it is the usual practice for the parents to arrange the marriage by finding a suitable partner for their children. It is not expected that the couple will be 'in love' when they marry. Love is expected to develop after marriage. The choice of marriage partner in Islam, Hinduism and Sikhism, must be of the same faith or someone who is converting to the faith.

In Christianity, it is usual for people to find their own marriage partner and hope that their parents will approve of their choice. The couple fall in love and then, as a sign of their love for each other, get married. A Christian is allowed to marry people of other faiths although it is recognised that problems may occur in the marriage if the religious beliefs and practices conflict. For example, some religious traditions allow the use of artificial methods of contraception and other religious traditions forbid it.

An arranged marriage is the accepted tradition in many religions

Questions ?

1 Explain how the teachings of **two** different Christian traditions might influence a married couple's decision about the use of contraception.
2 What is meant by an 'arranged marriage'?
3 Explain how the teachings of **two** religious traditions might guide parents in the choice of a marriage partner for their child.

What do you think? ?

1 Why do you think that Pope Paul VI condemned artificial methods of contraception but allowed Catholics to use the rhythm method as a means of controlling the size of their family?
2 What are Catholics using as a source of moral authority to decide whether or not to use artificial methods of contraception?

Marriage and divorce

Marriage

A Christian marriage ceremony is both a civil **contract** and a **covenant**. The couple are left in no doubt of the **commitment** and **responsibilities** that they are undertaking. At the beginning of the ceremony, they are reminded that the **three** purposes of marriage are:

- to provide each other with mutual help and support in both the bad as well as the good times

- to have sexual intercourse free from sin

- to have children who will be brought up in a Christian home.

During the marriage ceremony the Christian couple are making a commitment to each other for life. They are taking responsibility for each other and in the marriage vows they exchange the couple state these responsibilities. The following marriage vows may be found in the Alternative Service Book of the Church of England. During the service the vicar will ask the bride and groom in turn:

(Name), will you take (Name) to be your husband? Will you love him, comfort him, honour and protect him, and forsaking all others, be faithful to him as long as you both shall live?

The bride and groom will agree that:

I, (Name) take you (Name), to be my wife; to have and to hold; from this day forward; for better, for worse, for richer, for poorer, in sickness and in health, to love, and to cherish, till death us do part, according to God's holy law; and this is my solemn vow.

The ring that is exchanged during the marriage ceremony is symbolic of the Christian belief that marriage is for life.

I give you this ring as a sign of our marriage. With my body I honour you, all that I am I give to you, and all that I have I share with you, within the love of God, Father, Son and Holy Spirit.

Divorce

Many couples find that they can no longer live together and end their marriage by **divorce**.

The Divorce Reform Act 1971 allows a UK couple to have a divorce if the marriage has 'irretrievably broken down', but many Christians believe that even if they were to have a divorce, they would still be married in God's eyes. This would mean that they would be guilty of adultery if they married someone else. They base this belief on the teaching of Jesus.

What is...?

Commitment is a pledge or vow to do or be something.

A **contract** is a binding agreement.

A **covenant** is a binding agreement made in the presence of God.

A **responsibility** is a duty or duties one undertakes.

Activity

1 Summarise the commitment the couple make to each other in the marriage ceremony.

2 Summarise the responsibilities that the couple undertake for each other.

3 Explain why the marriage ceremony in the Church of England is not only a contract but also a covenant.

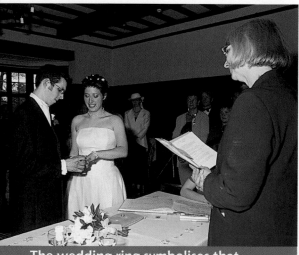

The wedding ring symbolises that marriage is for life

When asked if a couple could divorce, Jesus answered that God established marriage at the time of creation and a couple become 'one flesh' when they marry and only God can end that marriage.

'But in the beginning, at the time of creation, "God made them male and female," as the scripture says. "And for this reason a man will leave his father and mother and unite with his wife, and the two will become one." So they are no longer two, but one. No human being then must separate what God has joined together.'

When they went back into the house, the disciples asked Jesus about the matter. He said to them, 'A man who divorces his wife and marries another woman commits adultery against his wife.'
(Mark 10:6–12)

The Catholic Church does not accept divorce. In the eyes of the Catholic Church, the couple are married for life and to re-marry would be adultery. Catholics accept that God alone can end the marriage through the death of one of the partners. Even if a couple separate, they must remain celibate, as any other sexual relationship they might have would be adultery.

What God hath joined together, let man not separate

Occasionally, the Catholic Church allows an **annulment** of a marriage. An annulment is allowed if, for example, there has never been sexual intercourse between the couple. An annulment is not a divorce; it is the cancellation of a marriage.

The Church of England does not, in principle, accept divorce. The Church teaches that marriage is for life and their general policy is not to re-marry divorcees in a church ceremony. An increasing number of vicars are offering a blessing after the re-marriage of divorced people in a civil ceremony, and the Church of England is reviewing its attitude to the marriage of divorcees in church.

Many Free Churches, such as Quakers, believe that the community should seek to help the couple to overcome their difficulties. If divorces do happen then the couple should be allowed to re-marry in a church ceremony. These denominations believe that it is not physical death of one of the partners that ends the marriage. Rather, the marriage ends with the death of the love between the couple. These denominations believe that it is better for the couple to begin their new relationship with the blessing of the Church.

What is...?

An **annulment** in the Catholic Church is the declaration that the marriage never took place properly. It is not a divorce but a cancellation of the marriage.

A **divorce** is the legal termination of a marriage. After a divorce the couple are free to re-marry.

Activity

1 In small groups, make a list of the causes of stress in a marriage.

2 Report the list back to your teacher for a class list to be made.

3 Write down the complete list.

Questions ?

1 Explain why a Christian couple may wish to marry in a Church rather than a registry office.

2 State and explain **three** purposes of a Christian marriage.

3 Explain how the marriage vows show the commitment and responsibilities that the couple are undertaking.

4 What is the difference between an 'annulment' and a 'divorce'?

5 Explain the attitude of **two** Christian traditions to divorce.

Racial prejudice

What is...? 📖

Prejudice is a pre-judgment, a feeling and attitude people have towards an individual, a group, or a race of people before they know much about them. It is a biased opinion against someone or something for no logical reason. Prejudice is a feeling and attitude so it is an **emotion**.

Discrimination is putting prejudice into **action**. Discrimination means that an individual, a group, or race is treated differently because of the prejudice.

Stereotyping is a fixed mental image about a group. Stereotyping is the belief that all members of a group conform to the same pattern.

Racial prejudice is pre-judgment about a particular race – the belief that one group of people is inferior or superior to others based solely on their colour or race.

Genocide is the mass extermination of a particular race or nation.

One form of **prejudice** is against a particular race or religion. Scientifically there is no difference between races. Despite scientific research investigating and charting blood groups, bone structure and brain sizes, scientists have found no biological characteristics that belong exclusively to any one group of the world's people. In the past there have been attempts to define races to show one group as inferior or superior. The treatment of the Jews by the Nazis is one example.

The Nazi regime made a decision to rid the world of 'Jewish blood'. This was a form of **genocide**. It is estimated that 6 million Jews were killed as part of this policy. Many of the Jews died in the gas chambers in concentration camps such as Belsen and Auschwitz. The Jews call this event the 'Holocaust'.

The Nazi's 'Final Solution' shocked the world and yet racial prejudice still continues in the world today. More than 200,000 civilians were killed in the Bosnian war due to a process called ethnic cleansing. Ethnic cleansing is a process in which the advancing army of one ethnic group expels civilians of the other ethnic group from the towns and villages it conquers in order to create an area free of any other ethnic group other than their own. The Bosnian conflict was between Christians and Muslims.

The causes of **racial prejudice** include:

- fear that a particular race will take over a country

- fear that one group's cultural identity will be lost if another race is allowed to integrate into their society

- ignorance of the culture of another racial group, leading to misunderstandings.

Racial prejudice is illegal in Britain. The Race Relations Act 1976 makes it illegal to discriminate on the grounds of colour, race or nationality. It is illegal to discriminate in the fields of employment, housing, education, and the provision of goods, facilities and services. The Commission for Racial Equality was set up under the Race Relations Act to deal with complaints of **discrimination**.

Ethnic cleansing still happens

What do you think? ?

The extract below is from the letter of James in the New Testament. What instruction do you think James was giving to Christians?

You will be doing the right thing if you obey the law of the Kingdom, which is found in the scripture, 'Love your neighbour as you love yourself.' But if you treat people according to their outward appearance, you are guilty of sin, and the Law condemns you as a lawbreaker. (James 2:8–9)

Activity

The Old Testament teaches that God expects foreigners (aliens) staying in a country to be treated equally to those born in that country. God reminds the Jews of their treatment as slaves in Egypt:

'Do not ill-treat foreigners who are living in your land. Treat them as you would a fellow-Israelite, and love them as you love yourselves. Remember that you were once foreigners in the land of Egypt. I am the Lord your God.' (Leviticus 19:33–4)

1 Explain why God reminds the Jews of their time as slaves in Egypt when instructing them not to mistreat foreigners.

2 How might Christians in Britain apply this teaching to the treatment of immigrants?

Questions ?

1 **(a)** Explain the terms 'prejudice' and 'discrimination'.
  (b) Explain the difference between prejudice and discrimination.
2 Why do you think that laws are able to stop discrimination but not prejudice?
3 State **three** causes of racial prejudice.
4 What was the Holocaust?
5 What is ethnic cleansing?
6 Give reasons why you think the Holocaust and ethnic cleansing appear to be against God's teaching in Leviticus.

Teachings on racial prejudice 1

Some Christians look to the story of Adam and Eve as evidence that all races are descended from the same ancestors. God did not create different races of people at the time of creation, just one man and one woman. They believe that Genesis teaches that in God's eyes human beings belong to one family and racial prejudice is a sin.

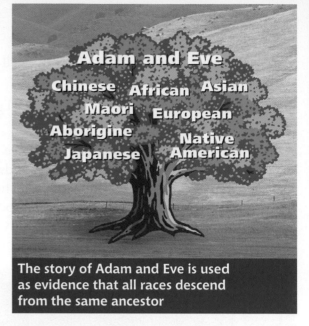

Adam and Eve

Chinese African Asian
Maori European
Aborigine
Japanese Native American

The story of Adam and Eve is used as evidence that all races descend from the same ancestor

Most Christians use the following passages as a source of moral authority. They teach that Christians should live in harmony with others and regard everyone as their neighbour, regardless of race and colour. There should be equality and justice for everyone.

When Jesus healed the Centurion's servant (opposite), he taught that it is possible for people of different races and religions to live together in harmony, respecting each other's beliefs. The Romans worshipped many gods, but the Jews only believed in the one God. Jews did not enter the homes of Gentiles (non-Jews) for fear of being made 'unclean' in a spiritual sense. This attitude might offend some people but the Centurion understood that it was part of their beliefs and was not offended.

Jesus told a parable involving a good Samaritan (see opposite) to teach that 'my neighbour' is everyone. Jesus had two supposed good men ignoring the needs of an injured man of their own race. The help comes from the man's supposed racial enemy.

What is...?

A **community** is a group of people who live together or come together for a special purpose. The community shares a common humanity or common beliefs and have a sense of responsibility for each other.

Equality is every human being having the same rights as any other human being.

Justice is to bring about what is right and fair according to the law, or is making up for what has been done wrong.

What is...?

A **parable** is a story. It uses everyday situations to teach people about an idea or a belief.

Activity

Before you read the Parable of the Good Samaritan, use the Internet and/or the library to find out why Samaritans and Jews were enemies at the time of Jesus.

Questions ?

1 Explain the terms 'community', 'justice' and 'equality'.
2 What does the incident of the healing of the Centurion's servant teach Christians about living in harmony with other races?
3 What does the Parable of the Good Samaritan teach a Christian about 'who is my neighbour'?
4 What do these two biblical passages teach Christians about the treatment of other races?

The incident of the Centurion's servant (Luke 7:1–10)

When Jesus had finished saying all these things to the people, he went to Capernaum. A Centurion there had a servant who was very dear to him; the man was sick and about to die. When the Centurion heard about Jesus, he sent some Jewish elders to ask him to come and heal his servant. They came to Jesus and begged him earnestly, 'He loves our people and he himself built a synagogue for us.'

So Jesus went with them. He was not far from the house when the Centurion sent friends to tell him, 'Sir, don't trouble yourself. I do not deserve to have you come into my house, neither do I consider myself worthy to come to you in person. Just give the order, and my servant will get well. I, too, am a man placed under the authority of superior officers, and I have soldiers under me. I order this one, "Go!" and he goes; I order that one, "Come!" and he comes; and I order my slave, "Do this" and he does it.'

Jesus was surprised when he heard this; he turned round and said to the crowd following him, 'I tell you, I have never found faith like this, not even in Israel!'

The messengers went back to the Centurion's house and found his servant well.

The Parable of the Good Samaritan (Luke 10:25–36)

A teacher of the Law came up and tried to trap Jesus. 'Teacher,' he asked, 'what must I do to receive eternal life?'

Jesus answered him, 'What do the Scriptures say? How do you interpret them?'

The man answered, '"Love the Lord your God with all your heart, with all your soul, with all your strength, and with all your mind"; and "Love your neighbour as you love yourself."'

'You are right,' Jesus replied; 'do this and you will live.'

But the teacher of the Law wanted to justify himself, so he asked Jesus, 'Who is my neighbour?'

Jesus answered, 'There was once a man who was going down from Jerusalem to Jericho when robbers attacked him, stripped him, and beat him up, leaving him half dead. It so happened that a priest was going down that road; but when he saw the man, he walked on by, on the other side. In the same way a Levite also came along, went over and looked at the man, and then walked on by, on the other side. But a Samaritan who was travelling that way came upon the man, and when he saw him, his heart was filled with pity. He went over to him, poured oil and wine on his wounds and bandaged them; then he put the man on his own animal and took him to an inn, where he took out two silver coins and gave them to the innkeeper. "Take care of him," he told the innkeeper, "and when I

The Samaritan helps the Jew who fell among thieves (Henry Coller)

come back this way, I will pay you whatever else you spend on him."'

And Jesus concluded, 'In your opinion, which one of these three acted like a neighbour towards the man attacked by the robbers?'

Teachings on racial prejudice 2

Activity

1 Read Jesus' teaching in Matthew 22:32–9.

2 Write a paragraph to explain how Jesus' teaching in Matthew 22:32–9 links with the teaching in the Parable of the Good Samaritan.

3 How might both these teachings be applied to the treatment of other races?

Activity

1 The class is to divide into groups of four or five pupils.

2 Each group is to research one of the Christians below. (Each group must choose a different Christian.)

- Trevor Huddleston
- Maximilian Kolbe
- Martin Luther King
- Nelson Mandella
- Desmond Tutu.

3 Each group is to research:

- the life and work of the Christian to combat racism
- why the Christian felt that they must work against racism
- the success of the Christian's work.

4 The group is to present their findings to the rest of the class.

5 Each member of the class is to make notes on the life and work of each Christian presented.

The early followers of Jesus believed that Christianity was only for Jews and therefore any Gentile (non-Jew) who wanted to become a Christian had to convert to Judaism first. This meant following the Jewish food laws. The vision of Peter (see opposite) changed this attitude. Peter baptised a Roman called Cornelius into the Christian faith. As a Roman Cornelius would not have followed the Jewish customs and would have eaten pork and other food, which the Jews believed were forbidden by God. When he became a Christian, Peter did not expect him to follow the Jewish food laws. This was because Peter believed that he had been shown in a vision that the Jewish food laws did not apply to Christians.

Peter's vision made him realise that to be baptised as a Christian did not require conversion to Judaism as well. In his vision Peter heard God saying that Christians need not keep the Jewish traditions and food laws. Peter realised that Gentiles were to be admitted into the Christian Church as well as Jews and that people do not have to change their culture and heritage when they accept the Christian faith, only their behaviour to meet the standards set by Jesus.

Combatting racial prejudice

As a result of biblical teaching, many Christian traditions actively fight racial prejudice.

The Catholic Church opposes racism. At the end of Vatican II, Pope Paul VI stated that racism was against Christ's teaching. He wrote that:

> *The Church reproves, as foreign to the mind of Christ, any discrimination against men or harassment of them because of their race, colour, condition of life or religion.*

He reminded Christians that St Peter had told them to 'maintain good fellowship among the nations' (1 Peter 2:12).

The Church of England agrees with the Catholic Church that racism is against Christian teaching. The Church teaches that it is part of their role to fight racism and works to strengthen relationships between the different faith communities within cities. The bishops of the Church of England have stated that they are committed to 'ensuring that all Church of England schools should seek to offer places to children of other faiths and of no faith in their local community'.

Quakers have felt led by the Holy Spirit to challenge racism, prejudice and discrimination. Quakers have a Social Justice Committee, which looks specifically at issues of racial justice and equal opportunities in all aspects of life. Quakers believe that they have a duty to end injustice caused by prejudice.

Peter's vision (Acts 11:1–18)

The apostles and the other believers throughout Judea heard that the Gentile also had received the word of God. When Peter went to Jerusalem, those who were in favour of circumcising Gentiles criticised him, saying, 'You were a guest in the home of uncircumcised Gentiles, and you even ate with them!' So Peter gave them a complete account of what had happened from the very beginning:

'While I was praying in the city of Joppa, I had a vision. I saw something coming down that looked like a large sheet being lowered by its four corners from heaven, and it stopped next to me. I looked closely inside and saw domesticated and wild animals, reptiles, and wild birds. Then I heard a voice saying to me, "Get up, Peter; kill and eat!" But I said, "Certainly not, Lord! No ritually unclean or defiled food has ever entered my mouth." The voice spoke again from heaven, "Do not consider anything unclean that God has declared clean." This happened three times, and finally the whole thing was drawn back up into heaven. At that very moment three men who had been sent to me from Caesarea arrived at the house where I was staying. The Spirit told me to go with them without hesitation. These six fellow-believers from Joppa accompanied me to Caesarea, and we all went into the house of Cornelius. He told us how he had seen an angel standing in his house, who said to him, "Send someone to Joppa for a man whose full name is Simon Peter. He will speak words to you by which you and all your family will be saved." And when I began to speak, the Holy Spirit came down on them just as on us at the beginning. Then I remembered what the Lord had said: "John baptised with water, but you will be baptised with the Holy Spirit." It is clear that God gave those Gentiles the same gift that he gave us when we believed in the Lord Jesus Christ; who was I, then, to try to stop God?'

When they heard this, they stopped their criticism and praised God, saying, 'Then God has given to the Gentiles also the opportunity to repent and live!'

Questions ?

1 Explain how Peter's vision showed that Christianity was no longer to be regarded as only for one racial group.
2 Explain the teaching of **two** religious traditions to racial prejudice.

Martin Luther King had a dream that one day there would be equality and justice for the black people of the USA

Activity

Look back at page 14 to remind yourself of what is meant by a conversion.

Look back at page 28 to remind yourself of how visions act as special revelation.

Activity

Look back to page 26. Remind yourself of how Vatican II and the General Synod of the Church of England act as sources of moral authority for Christians within those traditions.

Discrimination against women

The Suffragettes campaigned for women to be given the right to vote

Women have suffered prejudice and discrimination because of their **gender** for centuries. At the beginning of this century, it was believed that a woman's place was in the home looking after her husband and children. If women did the same work as men then women were paid less. Women were not given the same opportunities as it was believed that they could not work as efficiently as men or that they would leave to raise a family. Women did not have the right to vote, as men thought they would not understand politics.

Equal rights

Under the law of Britain, women are to have equal rights to men. The Equal Pay Act 1975 stated that women were to be paid on an

The incident of Mary and Martha (Luke 10:38–42)

As Jesus and his disciples went on their way, he came to a village where a woman named Martha welcomed him in her home. She had a sister named Mary, who sat down at the feet of the Lord and listened to his teaching. Martha was upset over all the work she had to do, so she came and said, 'Lord, don't you care that my sister has left me to do all the work by myself? Tell her to come and help me!'

The Lord answered her, 'Martha, Martha! You are worried and troubled over so many things, but just one is needed. Mary has chosen the right thing, and it will not be taken away from her.'

equal basis to men who do the same or broadly similar jobs. The Sex Discrimination Act 1975 made it illegal to suggest in an advertisement that a job was only for men or only for women. Women and men must be given equal opportunities for promotion within the workplace.

Jesus

Jesus was born into a society where women had a second-class role. Their husbands owned them. Jewish men thanked God daily in their prayers that they had not been born a woman. In a public place, a man would not acknowledge a woman, even his wife or daughter. Women were not allowed to worship God alongside men in the synagogue or temple in Jerusalem. Women had a separate area in which to worship.

Jesus' treatment of women contrasted with the accepted attitudes of the time. There are several incidents in the Gospels in which Jesus showed that he believed women were equal to men. It was women who discovered that Jesus had risen from the dead and one of the first people to see Jesus after the resurrection was Mary Magdalene. Luke's Gospel mentions that women as well as men accompanied Jesus on his travels. In his ministry, Jesus talked to and healed women as naturally as he did men.

Women did not sit with men for meals. The women would wait on the men and then eat in the kitchen. A rabbi would not teach women. In the incident of Mary and Martha (above), Jesus breaks this rule. He allows Mary to listen to his teaching.

On another occasion, Jesus spoke to a Samaritan woman (John 4:5–28). In this incident Jesus was not only showing that his teaching was for women as well as men, but also for all races.

Activity

1 Read the incident of Jesus and the Samaritan woman (John 4:5–27) on page 69.

2 Outline the incident in your own words.

3 Explain how this incident shows that Jesus' teaching was for both sexes and all races.

Jesus met a Samaritan woman at a well and spoke to her

The ordination of women

Dawn French as the vicar of Dibley

St Paul taught that Christians are all part of the same community because of their shared beliefs. For a Christian, there are no differences between the races and sexes, as everyone is equal before God.

It is through faith that all of you are God's children in union with Christ Jesus. You were baptised into union with Christ, and now you are clothed, so to speak, with the life of Christ himself. So there is no difference between Jews and Gentiles, between slaves and free people, between men and women; you are all one in union with Christ Jesus. If you belong to Christ, then you are the descendants of Abraham and will receive what God has promised. (Galatians 3:26–9)

Yet many women believe that St Paul did not believe in equality for women and did much to establish the view that women were to obey men. In 1 Timothy 2:9–15 St Paul said:

I also want the women to be modest and sensible about their clothes and to dress properly; not with fancy hair styles or with gold ornaments or pearls or expensive dresses, but with good deeds, as is proper for women who claim to be religious. Women should learn in silence and all humility. I do not allow them to teach or to have authority over men; they must keep quiet. For Adam was created first, and then Eve. And it was not Adam who was deceived; it was the woman who was deceived and broke God's law. But a woman will be saved through having children, if she perseveres in faith and love and holiness, with modesty.

His reason for this view was that Adam was made before Eve and it was Eve that had led Adam to commit the first (original) sin. St Paul's views on women would be called prejudice in Britain today.

Most Christians agree that Christianity is for both men and women, but not all Christian traditions agree on the role women can take in worship.

The Catholic and Orthodox Churches do not ordain women. Their reasons for not ordaining women include the following.

- Jesus did not make a woman one of the twelve Apostles so he did not intend women to take leadership roles.

- St Paul preached that women must obey their husbands and be silent in church. His teaching is understood to mean that God intended women to have subordinate roles in the Church's structure.

- The priest represents Christ during Holy Communion. As women menstruate each month, they are unfit to consecrate the bread and wine during Holy Communion and to represent Christ who was a man.

- The tradition of the all-male priesthood is an unbroken tradition that goes back to Jesus. The Church would be wrong to break this tradition.

The Church of England has accepted the ordination of women priests since 1994, but at the loss of many male priests who could not agree with the ordination of women. The reasons that the Church of England has ordained women include the following.

- God created both men and women in his likeness so there is no reason to suggest that he did not give them equality to take on all roles in society.

- Jesus gave women greater equality than his time permitted. If Jesus were alive today then he would have allowed women to enter the priesthood.

- Women feel called by God to be priests and should have the opportunity to answer the call.

- Galatians 3:28 teaches that men and women are to be treated equally.

- Many women in the early days of the Christian Church seem to have taken a priestly role.

Quakers believe that every person is capable of understanding the will of God and teaching it to others. In Quaker worship anyone who feels moved to speak may do so regardless of race or sex.

What is...?

Ordination is the service that makes an individual a leader in the Christian Church.

Questions ?

1 Why might St Paul's attitude to women appear outdated in today's world?
2 What is 'ordination'?
3 Why are Orthodox and Catholic churches opposed to the ordination of women?
4 Why does the Church of England now ordain women?
5 What is the Quaker view of the ordination of women?
6 'If Jesus had wanted women to be ordained, he would have chosen a woman apostle.' Do you agree? Give reasons for your answer, showing that you have thought about more than one point of view. Refer to religious teaching in your answer.

Do you understand ...

about the issues surrounding prejudice and discrimination?

Task 1

1 (a) Explain **two** examples of prejudice that might be found in Britain today.

 (b) Explain **two** examples of discrimination that might be found in Britain today.

2 Why do many Christians feel that they must work against racism?

3 Describe the work of one Christian who has opposed discrimination. In your answer, include examples of how the Christian opposed discrimination and how successful the Christian's opposition was in overcoming discrimination.

4 'Jesus was a racist.' Do you agree? Give reasons for your answer, showing that you have thought about more than one point of view. Refer to religious teachings in your answer.

Task 2

1 Explain why the Church of England allowed the ordination of women.

2 Choose another Christian tradition and outline its teachings against the ordination of women.

Angela Berners-Wilson was the first woman to be ordained as a priest in the Church of England in 1994

3 'Galatians 3:28 teaches that men and women are equal and we are "all one in union with Christ Jesus". Therefore, Christians who oppose the ordination of women are going against God.' Do you agree? Give reasons for your answer, showing that you have thought about more than one point of view.

Task 3

One day Jesus met a Samaritan woman at a well. Look back at your research from the activity on page 65 to remind yourself of the attitude of Jews to Samaritans. Remind yourself of the attitude of Jews to women at the time of Jesus by looking back at page 65.

1 Why do you think that the disciples were amazed to find Jesus 'talking with a woman'?

2 What do you think this incident teaches about prejudice and discrimination?

3 How might this incident be used to support the ordination of women?

Task 4

Look back at St Paul's teaching in 1 Timothy 2:9–15 on page 66 and read the passage below. Answer the following questions based on these two passages.

Wives, submit to your husbands as to the Lord. For a husband has authority over the church; and Christ is himself the Saviour of the church, his body. And so wives must submit completely to their husbands just as the church submits itself to Christ. (Ephesians 5:22–4)

1 Explain how St Paul's teaching led to the belief that women should not take leadership roles in the workplace.

2 Explain how St Paul's teaching supports the belief that women should not be ordained.

3 Why did St Paul believe that women were sinners?

4 How did St Paul believe that women could be saved from sin?

Jesus and the Samaritan woman (John 4:5–27)

In Samaria he came to a town named Sychar, which was not far from the field that Jacob had given to his son Joseph. Jacob's well was there, and Jesus, tired out by the journey, sat down by the well. It was about noon.

A Samaritan woman came to draw some water, and Jesus said to her, 'Give me a drink of water.' (His disciples had gone into town to buy food.)

The woman answered, 'You are a Jew, and I am a Samaritan – so how can you ask me for a drink?' (Jews will not use the same cups and bowls that Samaritans use.)

Jesus answered, 'If only you knew what God gives and who it is asking you for a drink, you would ask him, and he would give you life-giving water.'

'Sir,' the woman said, 'you haven't got a bucket, and the well is deep. Where would you get that life-giving water? It was our ancestor Jacob who gave us this well; he and his sons and his flocks all drank from it. You don't claim to be greater than Jacob, do you?'

Jesus answered, 'All those who drink this water will be thirsty again, but whoever drinks the water that I will give him will never be thirsty again. The water that I will give him will become in him a spring which will provide him with life-giving water and give him eternal life.'

'Sir,' the woman said, 'give me that water! Then I will never be thirsty again, nor will I have to come here to draw water.'

'Go and call your husband,' Jesus told her, 'and come back.'

'I haven't got a husband,' she answered.

Jesus replied, 'You are right when you say you haven't got a husband. You have been married to five men, and the man you live with now is not really your husband. You have told me the truth.'

'I see you are a prophet, sir,' the woman said. 'My Samaritan ancestors worshipped God on this mountain, but you Jews say that Jerusalem is the place where we should worship God.'

Jesus said to her, 'Believe me, woman, the time will come when people will not worship the Father either on this mountain or in Jerusalem. You Samaritans do not really know whom you worship; but we Jews know whom we worship, because it is from the Jews that salvation comes. But the time is coming and is already here, when by the power of God's Spirit people will worship the Father as he really is, offering him the true worship that he wants. God is Spirit, and only by the power of his Spirit can people worship him as he really is.'

The woman said to him, 'I know that the Messiah will come, and when he comes, he will tell us everything.'

Jesus answered, 'I am he, I who am talking to you.'

At that moment Jesus' disciples returned, and they were greatly surprised to find him talking with a woman. But none of them said to her, 'What do you want?' or asked him, 'Why are you talking to her?'

Citizenship Link

Using the Internet and/or library, research the following acts that aim to give all races and women equal rights in Britain.

- The Race Relations Act 1976
- The Equal Pay Act 1975
- The Sex Discrimination Act 1975

1 (a) Explain the key aspects of these three acts.

   (b) How successful do you think these acts have been in limiting racial discrimination and discrimination against women?

2 (a) What laws against racial discrimination is this poster supporting?

WHO SAYS ETHNIC MINORITIES CAN'T GET JOBS? THERE ARE OPENINGS EVERYWHERE.

   (b) How do the laws protect people against discrimination?

3 State **three** examples of gender discrimination against women that are against the law in Britain today.

World poverty

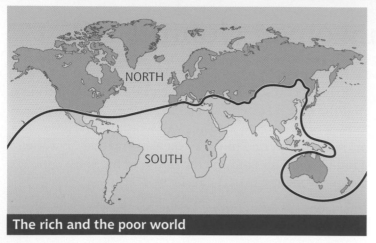
The rich and the poor world

The rich countries are often called the North, or the developed world. The poor countries are often called the South, or the developing world. Another name used to refer to the developing world is the Third World.

The problems found in the developing countries include:

- poverty
- hunger
- disease
- a population explosion.

Poverty

The developing world has only one fifth of the world's income to share between three quarters of the world's population. The outcome is poverty. As there is little industry in these countries, the main source of income for the population is farming. The majority of the farmers cannot produce enough food to feed their families and have no surplus to sell to make a profit. Poverty forms a vicious circle that is difficult to break.

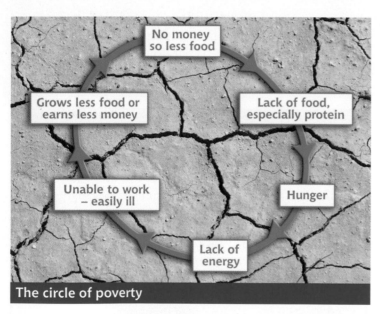
The circle of poverty

The circle of poverty shows that the problems of sickness, the inability to work, and malnutrition are linked. To overcome these, many countries have applied to the World Bank for financial help. But often the poor countries have no hope of repaying these debts. They have to spend a large amount of money just paying the interest owed.

Hunger

The causes of hunger in the developing world include the following.

- The climate results in too much or too little water for the crops. For example, drought was the cause of famine in Ethiopia, whereas there is frequent flooding in Bangladesh.

- The transportation of food from one area to another may be difficult. For example, poor roads or having to pass through war zones.

- Traditional farming methods cannot increase the yield from an area of land without damaging the soil.

- There are many diseases and pests in these countries that destroy crops and kill animals.

Disease

The problems of poverty, starvation and malnutrition in the developing world are the major causes of poor health. Children need more protein than adults because they are growing fast. If they do not get it, they can be harmed both physically and mentally. In the poorer countries, the death rate of children under five years is high. Children die because they are malnourished and lack resistance to disease. As a result of continuing poverty, poor health continues. The other causes of poor health in the developing countries include the following.

- Drinking water is in short supply or unfit to drink. The problem is greatest in heavily populated areas. Half the world's population do not have access to a clean and adequate water supply. 80 per cent of all the diseases of the world are water related.

- The people suffer from poor health, but they have less access to medical care than the people of developed countries. The lack of adequate medical care causes conditions to become worse, as patients often receive inadequate treatment.

- There are many insects that transmit diseases. For example, the mosquito spreads malaria.

- Few children are immunised against common ailments, such as measles, which can kill.

Population explosion

The annual increase in the population of the world mainly occurs in the developing countries. The rapid population growth in the poorest countries of the world means that any progress made in food production or healthcare is often lost. The causes of the population explosion in the developing world include the following.

- People tend to have large families to make sure that there are labourers to tend the land and someone to care for them in old age.

- The religious beliefs of many of these countries do not encourage the use of contraceptives.

- Recent improvements in medical care, nutrition and hygiene, have led to many more children surviving infancy.

- The improvement in medical care, nutrition and hygiene, has lowered the death rate in these countries so that more people are living longer.

Activity

Look back to pages 52–3 and remind yourself of the attitudes of different Christian traditions to the use of artificial contraception.

Questions ?

1 What other names are used to describe the countries of the North and the South?
2 (a) Name **two** countries in the North.
  (b) Name **two** countries in the South.
3 What are the **four** main problems found in the developing world?
4 What are some of the causes of poverty in the developing world?
5 What are some of the causes of hunger in the developing world?
6 What are some of the causes of poor health in the developing world?
7 What are the reasons for the population explosion becoming a problem in the developing world?

Caring for the poor

Mother Teresa helped the poor because she wanted to 'do something beautiful for God'

Religious believers are often very concerned with the problems of poverty and try to do all they can to help people in need around the world. Caring for the poor is an important part of Christian teaching and the Christian tradition has strong roots in helping those in need. Jesus was dedicated to helping those in need and Christians try to follow his example.

The passages on these two pages include some of the most important Christian teachings on wealth and poverty.

John the Baptist taught that people who want to do God's will must share what they have. He also taught that people should be content with their pay.

> *The people asked him, 'What are we to do, then?' He answered, 'Whoever has two shirts must give one to the man who has none, and whoever has food must share it.' Some tax collectors came to be baptised, and they asked him, 'Teacher, what are we to do?' 'Don't collect more than is legal,' he told them. Some soldiers also asked him, 'What about us? What are we to do?' He said to them, 'Don't take money from anyone by force or accuse anyone falsely. Be content with your pay.' (Luke 3:10–14)*

In the Parable of the Rich Fool, Jesus teaches the dangers of the pursuit of wealth. The farmer puts all his efforts into getting rich and when he thinks he can retire and enjoy his wealth, he dies. Someone else inherits all his possessions. The rich fool has done nothing that is of value in God's eyes. He has not built up 'treasures in heaven'. Jesus taught that people would not be judged on the size of their bank balance but on how they have helped those less fortunate.

In the Sermon on the Mount, Jesus warned that acts of charity should be from a genuine desire to help and should be done in secret.

> *Make certain you do not perform your religious duties in public so that people will see what you do. If you do these things publicly, you will not have any reward from your Father in heaven.*

> *So when you give something to a needy person, do not make a big show of it, as the hypocrites do in the houses of worship and on the streets. They do it so that people will praise them. I assure you, they have already been paid in full. But when you help a needy person, do it in such a way that even your closest friends will not know about it. Then it will be a private matter. And your Father, who sees what you do in private, will reward you. (Matthew 6:1–4)*

Questions ?

1 What did John the Baptist teach about helping the needy?

2 **(a)** Outline the Parable of the Rich Fool.

   (b) What does this parable teach about the use of wealth?

3 What did Jesus teach about the dangers of wealth in the Sermon on the Mount?

4 How might Christians put the teaching of John the Baptist and Jesus into practise by helping to overcome the problems of the developing world?

The Parable of the Rich Fool (Luke 12:13–21)

A man in the crowd said to Jesus, 'Teacher, tell my brother to divide with me the property our father left us.'

Jesus answered him, 'My friend, who gave me the right to judge or to divide the property between you two?' And he went on to say to them all, 'Watch out and guard yourselves from every kind of greed; because a person's true life is not made up of the things he owns, no matter how rich he may be.'

Then Jesus told them this parable: 'There was once a rich man who had land which bore good crops. He began to think to himself, "I haven't anywhere to keep all my crops. What can I do? This is what I will do," he told himself; "I will tear down my barns and build bigger ones, where I will store my corn and all my other goods. Then I will say to myself, Lucky man! You have all the good things you need for many years. Take

life easy, eat, drink, and enjoy yourself!" But God said to him, "You fool! This very night you will have to give up your life: then who will get all these things you have kept for yourself?"'

And Jesus concluded, 'This is how it is with those who pile up riches for themselves but are not rich in God's sight.'

Riches in heaven (Matthew 6:19–21)

Do not store up riches for yourselves here on earth, where moths and rust destroy, and robbers break in and steal. Instead, store up riches for yourselves in heaven, where moths and rust cannot destroy, and robbers cannot break in and steal. For your heart will always be where your riches are.

The rich young man (Mark 10:17–22)

As Jesus was starting on his way again, a man ran up, knelt before him, and asked him, 'Good Teacher, what must I do to receive eternal life?'

'Why do you call me good?' Jesus asked him. 'No one is good except God alone. You know the

commandments: "Do not commit murder; do not commit adultery; do not steal; do not accuse anyone falsely; do not cheat; respect your father and your mother."'

'Teacher,' the man said, 'ever since I was young, I have obeyed all these commandments.'

Jesus looked straight at him with love and said, 'You need only one thing. Go and sell all you have and give the money to the poor, and you will have riches in heaven; then come and follow me.' When the man heard this, gloom spread over his face, and he went away sad, because he was very rich.

Jesus repeated this teaching later in the Sermon when he warned that material possessions have no lasting value and the pursuit of wealth can often distract people from devotion to God. People need to build up 'treasures in heaven', not put their efforts into material things that might rust or be stolen. Jesus warned that people could not serve both 'God and money'.

Christians should be prepared to give everything they have to help others if God requests it. This is a very difficult thing to do, as a rich young man realised when he asked Jesus what he 'must do to inherit eternal life'. Jesus told him to keep the commandments and to sell everything that he had and give it to the poor. The rich young man could not do this as he was too attached to his wealth.

What do you think?

Look back at the Parable of the Good Samaritan on page 61. How do you think that Christians apply the teaching of this parable to helping the people in the developing world?

Perspectives on world poverty

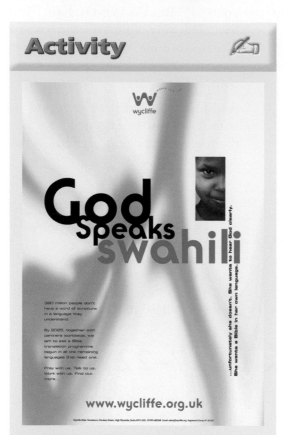
1 Using the Internet and/or library, research one of the following Christian organisations that helps the poor of the developing world:

- Christian Aid
- CAFOD/Trocaire
- Tear Fund.

2 Write a report of the work of the organisation you have researched. In your report, include:

- examples of the work they do
- examples of long-term aid
- examples of short-term aid
- how the organisation raises awareness
- how the organisation educates or campaigns for funds.

Kofi Annan, Secretary General of the United Nations, has stated that without debt cancellation, global poverty cannot be overcome

Christians agree that the Bible makes it clear that they have a duty to help those in need. Helping the developing world to overcome its problems is another way by which Christians can show 'love of their neighbour' and awareness that their neighbour is everyone in the world. However, there are some differences in the ways different Christian traditions think world poverty should be tackled.

After Vatican II, the Catholic Church decided that the Church should be closely involved with poor peoples' struggle for justice. This led to the development of Liberation theology (see page 37).

Not all Christians agree with Liberation theology because it has brought its supporters into conflict with the governments of many poor countries. Christians who oppose Liberation theology do not believe that helping the poor should not include becoming involved in politics. These Christians agree that Jesus taught compassion and expects Christians to give practical help to overcome the problems of the developing world, but this should not include direct involvement in politics. The Church of England for example,

Short-term aid is emergency aid at the time of a disaster

supports campaigns to reduce the debt poor countries have to pay rich countries and encourages its followers to give one per cent of their earnings to aid charities like Christian Aid. It advises the UK government on ethical issues relating to world poverty, but it does not actively work to change political situations within countries.

Aid

Many Christians believe that they can follow the teaching of Jesus by helping to raise money to support the work of charities seeking to overcome the problems of the developing world or by becoming involved in the work itself.

The help given might be long-term aid or short-term aid. Long-term aid seeks to overcome the problems of the developing world in such a way that help will not be needed in the future. It includes teaching people how to improve their farming methods and medical care. Short-term aid is emergency aid, the providing of supplies such as food and medical aid at the time of a disaster.

Questions ?

1 **(a)** How does Liberation theology apply to helping the poor?
   (b) Why do some Christians not agree with Liberation theology?
2 Explain the difference between long-term aid and short-term aid.
3 **(a)** Outline the work of a religious organisation that is seeking to overcome the problems of the developing world.
   (b) Why do many Christians believe that they should help to overcome the problems of the developing world? Refer to religious teaching in your answer.

about world poverty?

Task 1

Many Christians were involved with the millennium campaign, Jubilee 2000, to encourage rich countries to write off the debts of the poorer countries of the world. As a result of the campaign, many countries in the developing world received some debt relief. Jubilee Research is continuing the campaign's work. One of the main aims of the organisation is a 100 per cent cancellation of the debts of developing countries. Debt cancellation allows the governments of the developing world to divert money to help the poor of their country.

> *To be poor, is not to be able to satisfy basic human needs: food, housing, health, education, job and social participation. The Bible points out that to be poor is the same as to be 'oppressed'. (World Council of Churches)*

1 Explain the aim of Jubilee Research.

2 Why might the teaching of Jesus encourage Christians to support the work of Jubilee 2000 and Jubilee Research? Support your answer with reference to the teaching of Jesus.

Proclaim freedom to all the inhabitants of the land (Leviticus 25:10)

bring the money received from the sale, and hand it over to the apostles; and the money was distributed to each one according to his need.

And so it was that Joseph, a Levite born in Cyprus, whom the apostles called Barnabas (which means 'One who Encourages'), sold a field he owned, brought the money, and handed it over to the apostles. (Acts 4:34–7)

St Paul continued this teaching. He instructed the Christians of Corinth to share what they had.

Since you have plenty at this time, it is only fair that you should help those who are in need. Then, when you are in need and they have plenty, they will help you. In this way both are treated equally. As the scripture says, 'The one who gathered much did not have too much, and the one who gathered little did not have too little.' (2 Corinthians 8:14–15)

1 (a) Explain the attitude of the early Church to those in need.

   (b) What practical help did the members of the early Church give to those in need?

Task 2

The early Church put Jesus' teaching into practise by sharing all that they had to make sure that no one was in need. When Barnabas converted to Christianity, he sold his field and gave the money to those in need.

> *There was no one in the group who was in need. Those who owned fields or houses would sell them,*

2 Explain in detail how Christians might follow the example of the early Church in helping those in need in the developing world.

3 'Christians should not get tired of helping the poor.' Do you agree? Give reasons for your answer, showing that you have thought about more than one point of view. Refer to religious teaching in your answer.

The Parable of the Sheep and the Goats (Matthew 26:31–46)

'When the Son of Man comes as King and all the angels with him, he will sit on his royal throne, and the people of all the nations will be gathered before him. Then he will divide them into two groups, just as a shepherd separates the sheep from the goats. He will put the righteous people on his right and the others on his left. Then the King will say to the people on his right, "Come, you that are blessed by my Father! Come and possess the kingdom which has been prepared for you ever since the creation of the world. I was hungry and you fed me, thirsty and you gave me a drink; I was a stranger and you received me in your homes, naked and you clothed me; I was sick and you took care of me, in prison and you visited me."

'The righteous will then answer him, "When, Lord, did we ever see you hungry and feed you, or thirsty and give you a drink? When did we ever see you a stranger and welcome you in our homes, or naked and clothe you? When did we ever see you sick or in prison, and visit you?" The King will reply, "I tell you, whenever you did this for one of the least important of these members of my family, you did it for me!"

'Then he will say to those on his left, "Away from me, you that are under God's curse! Away to the eternal fire which has been prepared for the Devil and his angels! I was hungry but you would not feed me, thirsty but you would not give me a drink; I was a stranger but you would not welcome me in your homes, naked but you would not clothe me; I was sick and in prison but you would not take care of me."

'Then they will answer him, "When, Lord, did we ever see you hungry or thirsty or a stranger or naked or sick or in prison, and would not help you?" The King will reply, "I tell you, whenever you refused to help one of these least important ones, you refused to help me." These, then, will be sent off to eternal punishment, but the righteous will go to eternal life.'

Task 3

Read the Parable of the Sheep and the Goats above and answer the questions that follow.

1 Write out, in your own words, the Parable of the Sheep and the Goats.

2 Does this parable have anything to say about the problems of the developing world? Explain your answer.

3 To what extent is there a Christian solution for the developing world's problems? Give reasons for your answer.

I was hungry and you gave me something to eat

Citizenship Link

1 Using the Internet and/or library, research the World Bank and the International Monetary Fund (IMF).

2 Write a report to explain the work of each organisation.

3 (a) Why do you think some people believe that it is time to change to a fair trade system that will benefit the developing nation?

   (b) Why do you think that other people do not agree with such a change?

Conflict

What is...?

Conflict is a state of opposition, a fight or struggle.

Peace is living in harmony with one's neighbours, without any argument or hostility.

A **riot** is a civil disturbance that results in violent conflict. It is when a group of people 'disturbs the peace' by lawless conduct or behaviour. A riot is usually short lived and limited to one area of a country.

A **war** is an armed conflict between two opposing forces.

Terrorism is war waged by a group against a political or religious system. The terrorists use bombs, kidnapping, hijackings and shooting to fight for their cause. Terrorists often claim that they are forced to act as they do, because it is the only way to remove what they see as an evil political or religious system. An act of terrorism is not open warfare.

There was a riot in Bradford in 2001

The Middle East

The causes of conflict

There are many causes of riots, these include:

- one group feeling that it receives unfair treatment because of their race or colour
- in an area of poor housing or high unemployment, feelings of frustration exploding into a violent protest
- a disagreement between two opposing religious or political groups developing into a violent conflict.

A longer lasting conflict is a **war**. The causes of war include the following.

- One country invades another country because it is seeking to extend its territory or to gain specific resources found in that country. In 1991 Iraq invaded Kuwait to gain access to Kuwait's oil wells. This caused the Gulf War (1991).

- Countries go to war because they both claim ownership of a particular territory. In 1982 Britain and Argentina went to war over ownership of the Falkland Islands. The war began when Argentinean forces invaded the island to claim sovereignty. Britain sent a large task force to recapture the islands.

- A war seeks to stop the spread of a religious or political system. In the 1960s the USA became involved in the Vietnam War to stop the spread of Communism from North Vietnam into South Vietnam.

- A war may seek to overthrow a religious or political system. In 1971 a civil war in Pakistan developed because East Pakistan wanted independence. The result was the formation of the independent state of Bangladesh.

- Sometimes war is regarded as the lesser of two evils. It is felt that war will bring about a better situation than doing nothing. The USA dropped the only atomic bombs used in a war on the Japanese cities of Hiroshima and Nagasaki in August 1945. Despite the fact that the two bombs killed hundreds of thousands of civilians, the USA claimed that the use of the bombs brought the end of the war nearer and avoided further casualties.

The results of conflict

Any form of violent conflict has serious consequences including the following.

- War might lead to the development of an arms race, as nations ensure that they have sufficient military might to win the next war. Each time a nation improves its military capabilities, other nations believe that they have to do the same.

- Bloodshed through the injury and death of not only members of the military force but also civilians.

- Expense and debt, not only the cost of financing the war but also the repairing and rebuilding of damaged property after a riot or war.

- Refugees because many people who have escaped a war zone by going to another country are unable to return home after the war. Refugees have to be supported by the country in which they took refuge.

- Destruction of the environment.

- Shortages of food and goods.

The first atomic bomb was dropped on Hiroshima, Japan, on 6 August 1945

Activity

1 Look back to the explanation of the term 'sanctity of life' on page 40.

2 Write a paragraph to explain how a Christian might apply the idea of the sanctity of life to the morality of war.

Questions ?

1 (a) Explain how a riot is different from a war.
  (b) What causes people to riot?
  (c) Explain how the causes of a riot are different from those of a war.
2 What is 'terrorism'?
3 State **four** consequences of conflict.

Attitudes to conflict

Pacifists during a war are often called conscientious objectors

There is division within Christianity as to whether or not Christians should be involved in armed conflict. Some Christians believe that however just the cause, violence is never the solution. Quakers are Christians who oppose any form of violence. Their refusal to use violence is called the Quaker 'peace testimony'. Quakers believe that there is a part of God in all people and that this makes all human life sacred. They also believe that appealing to the part of people that is good will have better results than threatening people with violence or punishment. Quakers are **pacifists**.

Historically, pacifists have been regarded by some people as cowards and punished or rejected for refusing to fight in a war. Pacifists have proved that they are not cowards and undertaken such non-combatant roles as stretcher-bearers on the front line and ambulance drivers. During a war, pacifists are often called conscientious objectors.

Not all Christians agree with the Quakers' absolute position that war and the use of force is never justified. While all Christian traditions see war as evil, some accept that there are times when it is the lesser of two evils. So there is division within Christianity as to whether or not Christians should be involved in armed conflict. This is because the teaching of Jesus, the main source of moral authority for Christians, can be used to support either view – the pacifist views of Christians such as the Quakers and the views of Christians who feel believers should be able to fight for justice and against evil.

Christians who believe that it is acceptable to use force support their view with the New Testament account of the cleansing of the temple (Mark 11:15–18).

In this incident, people who came to worship at the temple in Jerusalem were being cheated in the temple courtyard, which was used as a marketplace. This made Jesus angry and he drove the traders out of the courtyard. This action brought Jesus into conflict with the authorities.

Jesus may have been angry that the priests, the very people who should have been helping them, were cheating the poor, or Jesus may have disapproved of the use of a religious building as a marketplace. Whatever his reasons, Jesus took action. Christians who use this incident to support their involvement in violent protest claim that Jesus took a violent action against the authorities when he saw injustice and so they must do the same. Christians who disagree with the use of violent protest argue that Jesus did not hurt anyone so it is not evidence that he agrees with the use of violence.

What is...?

Pacifism is the belief that war can never be justified; **pacifists** refuse to take part in war.

The arrest of Jesus (Matthew 26:50–3)

Then they came up, arrested Jesus, and held him tight. One of those who were with Jesus drew his sword and struck at the High Priest's slave, cutting off his ear. 'Put your sword back in its place,' Jesus said to him. 'All who take the sword will die by the sword. Don't you know that I could call on my Father for help, and at once he would send me more than twelve armies of angels?'

Revenge and love for enemies (Matthew 5:38–48)

You have heard that it was said, "An eye for an eye, and a tooth for a tooth." But now I tell you: do not take revenge on someone who wrongs you. If anyone slaps you on the right cheek, let him slap your left cheek too. And if someone takes you to court to sue you for your shirt, let him have your coat as well. And if one of the occupation troops forces you to carry his pack one kilometre, carry it two kilometres.

When someone asks you for something, give it to him; when someone wants to borrow something, lend it to him.

'You have heard that it was said, "Love your friends, hate your enemies." But now I tell you: love your enemies and pray for those who persecute you, so that you may become the children of your Father in heaven. For he makes his sun to shine on bad and good people alike, and gives rain to those who do good and to those who do evil. Why should God reward you if you love only the people who love you? Even the tax collectors do that! And if you speak only to your friends, have you done anything out of the ordinary? Even the pagans do that! You must be perfect – just as your Father in heaven is perfect!'

In Luke 22:36, Jesus instructs his followers to carry a sword:

'But now,' Jesus said, 'whoever has a purse or a bag must take it; and whoever has no sword must sell his coat and buy one.'

Some Christians also regard this as evidence that Jesus supported the use of violence on occasions. However, the argument comes back from Christians who deny the use of violence, that Jesus was telling his followers to carry a sword for their own protection.

When Judas and the authorities arrested Jesus, a disciple drew his sword to protect Jesus. Jesus stated that violence leads to violence and eventually death. Christians such as Quakers understand this to mean that they must not retaliate if attacked and believe that violence is going against God's will and is a sin. Other Christians argue that Jesus stopped the disciple because the action might lead to the disciple's death as the group was outnumbered.

In the Sermon on the Mount, Jesus stated that God would bless the peacemakers. In another section of the Sermon, he demonstrated how people live in harmony and avoid situations that lead to conflict. Jesus taught that God treats everyone in the same way, whether they are sinners or not. Christians must do the same.

Question ?

'Christians never take part in war.' Do you agree? Give reasons for your answer, showing that you have thought about more than one point of view. Refer to religious teaching in your answer.

81

Just war

What is...?

A **just war** is a war fought for a just cause (or according to the principles of a just war).

Activity

1 Look back to page 60.

2 Explain the term 'justice'.

3 How might Christians apply the idea of justice to arguments about the morality of war?

Activity

1 Using the Internet and/or library, research one of the following wars that some Christians regard as a just war:

- World War II

- The Falklands War

- The Gulf War (1991).

2 Explain why this war might be thought to have met the criteria of a just war.

Questions

1 How did St Paul expect the enemy to be treated?

2 Why did St Paul teach that the authority of the state should be obeyed?

3 Explain the concept of a 'just war'.

4 **(a)** Outline the details of a twentieth-century war that you consider to be just.

   (b) Explain why you consider this war to be just.

The early Christians suffered persecution and many were put to death. St Paul taught that Christians must leave revenge for their treatment to God. Christians must do everything to keep the peace and not give in to evil. Rather than harm an enemy, a Christian must give him food and water. In this way the enemy will feel shame for his actions.

> *If someone has done you wrong, do not repay him with a wrong. Try to do what everyone considers to be good. Do everything possible on your part to live in peace with everybody. Never take revenge, my friends, but instead let God's anger do it. For the scripture says, 'I will take revenge, I will pay back, says the Lord.' Instead, as the scripture says: 'If your enemies are hungry, feed them; if they are thirsty, give them a drink; for by doing this you will make them burn with shame.' Do not let evil defeat you; instead, conquer evil with good. (Romans 12:17–21)*

St Paul instructed Christians to obey the ruling authority because God has put them there. If the ruler is disobeyed then God is disobeyed. The authority is there for everyone's protection and there is nothing to fear if one keeps the laws. St Paul instructs Christians to respect the laws and pay their taxes. If the laws are broken then it is only right that an individual is punished. However, no ruling authority is entitled to ask a Christian to go against their conscience. This has led some Christians to think that under those circumstances they can protest.

St Paul's instruction to care for the enemy and to be obedient to the ruling authority has led some Christians to argue that if the ruling authority tells them to fight in a war then they must obey that command. Some Christians argue that war may be the lesser of two evils. There may be a worse evil, which only a war can defeat. These Christians believe that under certain carefully defined circumstances, war is allowed. This is called a **just war** ('just' meaning right or fair – like 'justice'). The just war theory seeks not only to justify war but also to limit it.

The thirteenth-century monk St Thomas Aquinas first established the just war theory. The conditions for a just war may be summarised as follows.

1 A just war can only be waged as a last resort. All non-violent options must have been tried before the use of force can be justified.

2 A war is just only if a legitimate ruling authority wages it. Even just causes cannot be served by actions taken by individuals or groups who do not have the support of the state or ruler.

3 A just war can only be fought to promote good and overcome an evil. For example, self-defence against an armed attack is always considered a just cause.

Duties towards the state authorities (Romans 13:1–7)

Everyone must obey the state authorities, because no authority exists without God's permission, and the existing authorities have been put there by God. Whoever opposes the existing authority opposes what God has ordered; and anyone who does so will bring judgement on himself. For rulers are not to be feared by those who do good, but by those who do evil. Would you like to be unafraid of those in authority? Then do what is good, and they will praise you, because they are God's servants working for your own good. But if you do evil, then be afraid of them, because their power to punish is real. They are God's servants and carry out God's punishment on those who do evil. For this reason you must obey the authorities – not just because of God's punishment, but also as a matter of conscience.

That is also why you pay taxes, because the authorities are working for God when they fulfil their duties. Pay, then, what you owe them; pay them your personal and property taxes, and show respect and honour for them all.

4 A war can only be just if it is fought with a reasonable chance of winning and the minimum amount of force must be used to gain victory.

5 The ultimate goal of a just war is to re-establish peace. Peace must be made as soon as victory is gained.

6 Innocent civilians are never permissible targets of war and every effort must be taken to avoid killing civilians.

Saddam Hussein's invasion of Kuwait led to the Gulf War (1991)

George Bush, Senr., was the President of the USA during the Gulf War (1991)

Holy war

Syria and the Holy Land at the time of the Crusades

The early Christians believed in non-violence and did not retaliate when persecuted. They obeyed Jesus' teaching to 'turn the other cheek'. Later, some Christians developed the idea that, at times, God's cause has to be defended. This is a **holy war**; a war fought on behalf of God and supported by God.

A holy war is related to the just war theory in that war and violence are justified as ways of restoring peace and justice. However, some of the conditions are different and any one of the following conditions apply for a war to be a holy war:

- the leader of a holy war has to be a religious leader, not just any ruler or authority in the country. The leader may sometimes believe he or she has been directed by God to start a holy war.

- a holy war can be an aggressive war – an 'unprovoked' war to spread the faith. A just war is one that seeks to overcome evil. Advocates of a holy war do tend to see unbelief as an evil in itself.

- a holy war can be about recovering sacred places that have been taken over by another faith.

- a holy war can be about taking back whole countries that are now occupied by someone else – even if the country does not have any of the faith's believers living in it any more.

- a holy war can be started to get revenge for things done to another faith against believers.

Those who fight for a holy war are often told God will reward them in some way. Taking part in a holy war is often seen as a very spiritual thing, fighting alongside God or in God's name.

The Crusades

The Crusades is an example of a holy war.

After the fall of the Roman Empire, Christianity lost control over the Holy Land – the sacred places where Jesus had lived and died. By the Middle Ages, the Holy Land was largely under Muslim control. The first Crusade (there were nine in total) began in 1095 CE when Pope Urban II urged his followers to go and recover the Holy Land for Christianity, to rescue Christians from Muslim occupation and to revenge all those Christians who had been badly treated by the Muslims. The Pope said that this was 'the will of God'. All those who took part would be 'the soldiers of God'. They would have all their sins forgiven and receive a huge spiritual reward. The Crusaders wore a cross on their breastplate to show that they were fighting for God and Christ.

The Pope's call to arms was a huge success and thousands of men set out. After months of travelling and fighting, Jerusalem was captured and looted. Many of the citizens of Jerusalem were slaughtered, including many Jews.

Although the First Crusade did achieve the purpose of taking control of Jerusalem (for a while), historians are generally not very impressed by the war. A lot of the Christian nobles who went to the Crusades made a lot of money and grabbed a lot of land. The major Christian cities seemed most pleased about getting control over trade with the Middle East, rather than their spiritual regard. Many knights were so impressed by the culture and skills of their Muslim enemies, they copied their behaviour, which worried the Church and led to persecutions. And the behaviour of the Crusaders was often barbaric and shameful. The legacy of the Crusades still affects the relationship between the West and the Arab world today.

A crusading knight kneeling in prayer

What is...?

A **holy war** is a war fought for a religious purpose: a war 'in the name of God' or with 'God on your side'.

Questions ?

1 Explain the term 'holy war'.
2 In what ways did the Crusades meet the conditions of a holy war?
3 Did the Crusades meet the requirements for a 'just war'?
4 'If there were no religions, there would be no wars.' Do you agree? Give reasons for your answer, showing that you have thought about more than one point of view. Refer to religious teaching in your answer.

Do you understand …

about war and peace?

Task 1

Martin Luther King was a Christian pacifist who believed that any form of violent protest was wrong. He taught his followers to 'turn the other cheek' whatever violence was meted out to them. Even when his house was bombed, he refused to seek revenge.

1 What is a 'pacifist'?

2 What do you think that Martin Luther King meant when he said: 'Darkness cannot drive out darkness; only light can do that. Hate cannot drive out hate; only love can do that'?

3 Outline the teachings that might help a Christian pacifist to decide that violent protest is wrong. You may use teachings from sacred texts and statements made by authorities of the Christian tradition.

'Darkness cannot drive out darkness; only light can do that. Hate cannot drive out hate; only love can do that.'

Task 2

Dietrich Bonhoeffer was a German Lutheran pastor and theologian. The beginning of his ministry coincided with the rise of the Nazi party in Germany. Bonhoeffer first preached pacifism and non-violent protest against Hitler. When he realised what was happening to German Jews, he helped to organise escape routes for them into Switzerland. He was caught and imprisoned for his activities.

When Bonhoeffer realised that Hitler was not going to listen to peaceful protests, he joined the conspirators working for the overthrow of the Nazi regime. He

Dietrich Bonhoeffer (1906–45)

took part in the failed plot to assassinate Hitler and was imprisoned in Buchenwald concentration camp. He was executed on 9 April 1945. Bonhoeffer was a pacifist who came to believe that although violence is evil, there are worse evils, which can only be dealt with by the use of force.

In a letter, Bonhoeffer wrote:

> *Only the one for whom the final standard is not his reason, his principles, his conscience, his freedom, his virtue, but who is ready to sacrifice all these, when in faith and sole allegiance to God he is called to obedient and responsible action: the responsible person, whose life will be nothing but an answer to God's question and call.*

1 What did Bonhoeffer believe must be an individual's guide to a course of action?

2 What Christian teaching might have guided Bonhoeffer in his decision to support the plot to assassinate Hitler?

3 Why might some Christians believe that the plot to assassinate Hitler was going against the teaching of St Paul related to the authority of the state?

4 Why might other Christians believe that the teaching of St Paul supported Bonhoeffer's action?

5 'Non-violent protests never work.' Do you agree? Give reasons for your answer, showing that you have thought about more than one point of view. Refer to religious teachings in your answer.

Task 3

1 What is 'terrorism'?

2 Some terrorists believe that they are fighting a just war. Is it possible for a terrorist to fight a just war? Support your answer with reference to the conditions required for a just war.

3 Some terrorists believe that they are fighting a holy war. Is it possible for a terrorist to fight a holy war? Support your answer with reference to the conditions required for a holy war.

Terrorists destroyed a nightclub in Bali

Citizenship Link

The United Nations (UN) was set up in 1945 with the central function of persuading countries to resolve their differences without resorting to violence. If need be, the UN is able to raise armed forces from its member countries to fight aggression. The main UN peacekeeping body is the Security Council. It is made up of five permanent members: the UK, USA, Russia, France and China, with ten others elected every two years by the Assembly. The five permanent members have the power to 'veto' any decision of the Council.

1 Do you think that it is right for the permanent members of the Security Council to have 'veto' powers?

2 In what ways do you think that the UN helps to preserve world peace?

3 Do you think that an organisation such as the UN makes a difference in keeping the peace?

4 Why do you think that the UN fails on occasions to keep the peace?

5 Using the Internet and /or library, find out more about the work of the UN.

Damage to the environment

Smoke from power stations in Britain can cause acid rain in Sweden

There are many ways by which the natural world is being destroyed. These include:

- The greenhouse effect caused by the build up of carbon dioxide in the atmosphere, which traps the heat radiated from the Earth and the sun. This results in a rise in the earth's temperature (global warming). Some scientists believe that the long-term effect is extreme weather conditions. The worst consequence of global warming could be the melting of the ice caps at both poles. If the sea levels rise, many areas would become flooded and farming land lost.

- The ozone layer above the earth filters the ultraviolet rays of the sun. A hole has appeared in the ozone layer above Antarctica. In other parts of the world, the layer is very thin. A decline in global ozone levels endangers the health of the world's population. Increased ultraviolet radiation increases the risk of skin cancer. The major ozone depleting chemicals are CFCs and other synthetic chemicals.

- Acid rain is caused by some of the harmful chemicals that are present in the air. Some of the chemicals are produced by nature itself, such as by volcanoes. The majority are by-products of industrial processes, such as electricity production from the burning of fossil fuels like coal and oil. Waste gases from these processes may contain sulphur dioxide and nitrogen oxides. When these gases reach the atmosphere and combine with rain, they convert to sulphuric and nitric acid. The resulting acid rain destroys trees and pollutes rivers.

- Industrial waste can take many forms and is a cause of much of the pollution in the seas and rivers. The waste may be nuclear waste from power stations or toxic waste from manufacturing processes. Sewage discharges, farm pesticides and oil, are other pollutants of the oceans and rivers. The pollution not only kills fish and other sea creatures, but also can enter the human food chain.

- Our modern lifestyle in the Western world has resulted in the diminishing of the world's resources so quickly that they could run out. Many non-renewable resources that are thought to be running out include oil, gas and many minerals.

Deforestation

There is a growing concern that the rainforests are disappearing at a rate that could cause them to be destroyed within the next fifty years. Timber has been used for centuries to build furniture, houses and ships, but re-planting ensured that there was no significant reduction in the world's forests. In recent years, forests have been destroyed on a large scale. Threats to the earth by deforestation include the following.

- The change in the natural habitat of plants and animals has led to the near or total extinction of a number of animals and plants.

- The loss of plants and animals that could provide new cures for diseases or new crops to feed the starving people of the world.

Extinction

Deforestation is not the only cause of some species of animals coming close to extinction. The ivory, skin and fur trades have led to the poaching of many animals. Rhinos and elephants are killed annually for their tusks in Africa. Chinchillas, seals, tigers and leopards, have become endangered species because of the skin and fur trade.

Experts warn of the dangers to the Earth of deforestation

Over-hunting is another cause. The blue whale is close to extinction because whales are a popular source of meat and other products in Japan. Large numbers of dolphins drown each year because they become trapped in the nets intended to catch tuna. Over-fishing of the seas as well as pollution from toxic waste is reducing the world's fish stocks.

The hunting of animals is regarded as sport. In Britain, badger-baiting is illegal but it still takes place. The high-powered weapons available to hunters, means that the number of animals killed during the hunting season have increased significantly. Other animals are harmed through the increasing number of water sports. For example, the use of speedboats throughout the Florida Everglades has brought the manatee close to extinction. There is a growing concern that some species will survive only in zoos.

Questions ?

1 Explain **three** ways in which the world is being damaged.
2 Why do some people campaign to stop deforestation?
3 Explain **three** causes of some animals being brought close to extinction.
4 'Each generation has a duty to care for the environment for the sake of their children.' Do you agree? Give reasons for your answer, showing that you have thought about more than one point of view.

Caring for the natural world

Activity

Look back to page 54 and write a definition of the term 'responsibility'.

What is...?

Stewardship is the special responsibility God has given humans for the created world; the responsibility to care for the world on behalf of God.

Dominion means to have authority over something. The book of Genesis says that humankind was given 'dominion' over the world.

Creation is the created world, the environment.

Conservation is preserving the natural environment by taking steps to conserve natural resources.

Farmers are told they should keep the land fallow every seventh year to give the soil a chance to recover

There is an instruction from Deuteronomy 22:6 to care for birds

The first book of the Bible is Genesis. The word 'genesis' means 'origin'. Christians believe that Genesis contains an account of the **creation** (origin) of the universe by God. In the Genesis story, God created the universe out of nothing. This is followed by the creation of the earth, on which all kinds of plants, trees, life in the sea, birds in the air, and animals on the land developed. The final life form to appear was human.

Christians believe that God is the creator and 'the world and all that is in it belong to the Lord; the earth and all who live on it are his' (Psalm 24:1). Christians, together with many other religious believers, accept that God placed humankind in charge of his creation. Genesis states that humankind was given **dominion** over the world. In today's world, Christians understand this to mean that God's creation is on loan to people. Humans were put in charge and are responsible for the environment (**stewards**), which reflects God's greatness.

> *You appointed them rulers over*
> *everything you made;*
> *you placed them over all creation:*
> *sheep and cattle, and the wild animals too;*
> *the birds and the fish*
> *and the creatures in the seas. (Psalm 8:6–8)*

In today's world, Christians understand this to mean that God's creation is on loan to people. Humans, as stewards of the world, will one day have to account to their 'master' (God) on the way in which they have treated his property.

At several points in the Bible God instructed humans how to care for the environment.

> *'For six years sow your field and gather in what it produces. But in the seventh year let it rest, and do not harvest anything that grows on it. The poor may eat what grows there, and the wild animals can have what is left. Do the same with your vineyards and your olive trees.' (Exodus 23:10–11)*

What do you think? ?

Read the account of creation found in Genesis 1 on page 9. The writer of Genesis states that when he had finished, 'God looked at everything he had made, and he was very pleased'. Do you think that God would look at his creation today and be 'pleased'? Give reasons for your answer.

'When you are trying to capture a city, do not cut down its fruit trees, even though the siege lasts a long time. Eat the fruit, but do not destroy the trees; the trees are not your enemies.'
(Deuteronomy 20:19)

The instruction in Deuteronomy is to care for the trees; this could be applied to the destruction of the rainforests.

Catholics are taught that they have a duty of care of the environment and that they are stewards of the planet who will have to account to God for the care of it. Caring for the environment is an act of worship because Catholics believe it is a way of doing God's work. The Synod of Catholic Bishops (1971) published a report called 'Justice in the World' in which attention was drawn to the rich nations' exploitation of natural resources and dumping of waste in poorer countries. The Pope also called for a moral response to the whole environment and planning for future generations through a balanced policy between conservation and consumption in an encyclical called 'On Social Concern' (1988).

The Church of England shares the Catholic Church's view that humans are stewards of the planet and has published various reports to urge the government to take action to protect the environment. The first report to be issued was 'Man in his Living Environment' (1970). The General Synod (1992) passed a motion to urge the government to take steps to:

- establish a just and economical use of the earth's energy resources and to minimise the impact of consequential environmental pollution

- curtail damage to flora and fauna by human activities in this country and seek to extend such restraint elsewhere in the world

- consider what contribution it can make to the encouragement of the stabilising of the world's population so that human beings can live in sustainable harmony with the rest of the natural order and flourish without want.

Quakers agree that the world and everything in it are gifts from God for which people must care. Quakers are taught that the world that they pass on to the next generation should be at least as good as when they received it.

What do you think? ?

Why do you think that CAFOD believes that as Christians they must 'strive to be good stewards of all the resources entrusted to us, openly accountable for our work'?

Activity

As a result of the belief that they have a duty to protect the environment, many Christians work to overcome the destruction of the natural world. Some Christians believe that it is sufficient to work in their local environment to improve things, for example, through recycling schemes. Other Christians join local, national or international organisations that seek to improve the environment.

Using the Internet and/or library, research the work of a conservation organisation that Christians might join such as Greenpeace or Friends of the Earth. Write a report that explains:

- why the organisation was founded

- the aims of the organisation

- examples of the specific activities of the organisation.

Greenpeace works to preserve the environment for future generations

Animal rights

Is it ever right to eat meat?

Animal rights activists protest outside a pharmaceutical firm

In the Genesis account of creation, Adam named the animals. In the past, this led some Christians to believe that God had placed animals in the world for their use with no concern of how they were to be treated. Now, most Christians agree that God wishes humans to look after his creation as stewards, and this includes treating animals with respect. In Proverbs 12:10 it says: 'Good people take care of their animals, but wicked people are cruel to theirs.'

Animal testing

Part of the debate as to whether animals have rights includes the use of animals in scientific experiments. Most Christians object to the use of animals in cosmetic testing. However, most Christians support the use of animals in scientific experiments to find medical cures that could reduce human pain and suffering and save human life. Even though they agree with their use in experiments, these Christians would want the animals used in research to be cared for and respected.

The Catholic Church does not oppose animal testing: 'provided they remain within reasonable limits, medical and scientific experiments on animals are morally acceptable since they may help to save human lives or advance therapy' (Catholic Bishop's Conference). The new Catechism of the Catholic Church states that, 'Animals, like plants, and inanimate beings, are by nature destined for the common good of past, present and future humanity.' Later it states that animals 'may be used to serve the just satisfaction of man's needs'.

The Catechism urges people to proceed with kindness and gentleness towards animals, but the Catholic Church stresses that human lives are more important so it is more important to try to help humans who are suffering even if it is at the expense of animals. However, the animals used are owed respect and appropriate care.

The Church of England has also stated that animal testing can be justified for vital medical research. The Church of England has said 'that we believe that human beings have more value than animals. But the fact that we minimise the pain, suffering, distress or lasting harm that animals may have to undergo, shows that we regard them as having intrinsic value.'

Quakers prefer to allow the individual members to come to their own conclusions about the morality of animal experimentation, but they are generally tolerant towards those individuals who do support it. Many Quakers have been involved in peaceful campaigns against animal testing. There is no tradition of authoritative statements from the organising body of Quakers and there are Quaker medical researchers who hold Home Office licences to experiment on live animals. They would justify their actions by citing the beneficial results which can be achieved for humans and other animals.

Many Christians opposed to the use of animals in experiments say it degrades those who carry them out and should not be permitted. They suggest that advances in knowledge and technology do not require the use of animals, as computers are able to simulate the human response.

Vegetarianism

As with animal testing, Christians are divided as to whether or not it is acceptable in God's eyes to eat meat or other animal products.

Many Christians believe that God gave us animals for food and clothing, and argue that in Genesis 1:29–30, God told Adam that he has given him the animals and birds as food. Later, in Genesis 9:2–3, God says:

> *'All the animals, birds, and fish will live in fear of you. They are all placed under your power. Now you can eat them, as well as green plants; I give them all to you for food.'*

Both the Catholic Church and the Church of England believe that the killing of animals for food and other products is acceptable.

Other Christians oppose the eating of meat and argue that dominion does not mean that we have the right to conquer and exploit animals. Immediately after God gave people dominion over animals, they argue, he prohibited their use for food when he said, 'I have provided all kinds of grain and all kinds of fruit for you to eat' (Genesis 1:29). They argue that dominion means guardianship or stewardship, that is, being co-workers with God in taking care of and improving the world. What seems to be the point is that if we unnecessarily kill an animal, we will be accountable to God.

Many Quakers are vegetarian, as they believe that there is a part of God in the animals as well as humans. These Christians apply the sanctity of life to animals as well as to humans. Some Christians do not believe in using any animal products. They do not eat eggs or drink milk or wear anything made of leather because they see animal life as sacred.

What do you think? ?

> *It's all the same to them whether they kill a bull as a sacrifice or sacrifice a human being. (Isaiah 66:3)*

Why do you think many vegetarian Christians use the following passage from the Old Testament to support their view? How might some Christians use this passage to oppose animal testing?

Activity

Look again at the meaning of the term 'sanctity of life' on page 40.

Look again at the biblical passages on pages 90–1.

Write a paragraph to explain why a belief in the sanctity of life might lead some Christians to become vegetarians.

Write a second paragraph to explain why other Christians believe God allows the use of animals for food so long as they are treated with respect.

Questions ?

1 Explain the term 'vegetarianism'.
2 (a) Explain the terms 'sanctity of life' and 'dominion'.
  (b) How might **two** Christian traditions apply each of these ideas to arguments about the right and wrong use of animals as food?
3 'If God had not wanted us to eat meat he would not have given us canine teeth.' Do you agree? Give reasons for your answer, showing that you have thought about more than one point of view. Refer to religious teaching in your answer.

Do you understand ...

about the natural world?

Task 1

1 Outline some of the ways in which pollution is destroying the Earth.

2 Outline teachings that might help a Christian to decide how to use the Earth's resources. You may use teachings from the Bible and statements made by the Christian authorities.

3 'It is no good trying to save the rainforests as this means putting thousands of people out of work.' Do you agree? Give reasons for your answer, showing that you have thought about more than one point of view. Refer to religious teachings in your answer.

Task 2

All things of creation are children of the Father and thus brothers of man ... God wants us to help animals, if they need help. Every creature in distress has the same right to be protected.'
(St Francis of Assisi)

1 What does this quote from St Francis of Assisi tell you about his attitude to the treatment of animals?

2 What reasons do you think he would give to oppose the use of animals in experiments? Support you answer with religious teaching.

3 What reasons might other Christians give to support the use of animals in experiments? Support your answer with religious teaching.

Task 3

1 Explain the reasons a Christian vegetarian would give for not eating meat.

2 Why do other Christians state that meat eating is part of God's plan for humans?

3 Which view do you support? Give reasons for your view.

Industrial waste is harming the environment

Meat still forms an important part of many people's diet

Task 4

'Aren't five sparrows sold for two pennies? Yet not one sparrow is forgotten by God.' (Luke 12:6)

1 What do you think Jesus was teaching in this statement?

2 How do you think that this passage influences Christians to believe animal's have rights?

3 Why do other Christians accept that animals have the right of protection but not to the same rights as humans?

What is...?

'**Slash and burn**' is a means of clearing forests quickly to release land for crop growing.

The practice of 'slash and burn' is destroying the environment

Citizenship Link

Read the following information and answer the questions that follow.

Forests are important to provide:

• fuel and timber

• paper to meet the demand for newspapers, junk mail and writing paper

• a barrier to stop soil erosion by the wind

• a suitable environment for many forms of animals and plants

• oxygen through photosynthesis that supports life

• medicine, as one in four of all medicines come from the rainforests. The loss of these medicines could stop treatments for diseases like cancer.

In recent years, forests have been destroyed on a large scale. Commercial operations use logging, bulldozing and burning, to clear land for agriculture, cattle, and commercial tree plantations. In the developing world, this is known as '**slash and burn**'.

The land released for farming by 'slash and burn' is soon over-cultivated or over-grazed and the soil becomes unsuitable for farming. More land is needed so another area of the forest is cleared. The region, which was once lush green forest, becomes an arid desert. Every year an area about one third of the size of Britain becomes a desert in this way. Other forests are cleared to make way for roads and cities.

Tree-burning on a large scale releases millions of tons of carbon dioxide and raises the earth's temperature by an estimated three degrees centigrade. Deforestation also means that there are fewer trees to absorb carbon dioxide. The destruction of the rainforests is making a significant contribution to global warming.

At the United Nations 'Earth Summit' in Rio de Janeiro (1992), an international agreement (Agenda 21) was made to work together to promote sustainable development around the world. Local Agenda 21 is part of this global plan and asks local people how they think their immediate environment could be improved. Agenda 21 is based on the slogan, 'Think globally, act locally.'

1 Why should people in the UK be concerned at the loss of the rainforests?

2 What is Agenda 21?

3 The slogan of Agenda 21 is: 'Think globally, act locally.' What actions can be undertaken to help reduce deforestation locally by:

(a) individuals

(b) local authorities?

The nature of truth

Galileo was the first astronomer to use a telescope

What is...?

A **hypothesis** is a theory put forward as a starting point for further investigation to prove whether or not a theory is true.

Objective evidence is real evidence and not based on personal opinion. A theory based on personal opinion would be **subjective**.

Activity

1 Read page 6 and make a list of the different ways by which people prove things exist.

2 Write a paragraph to explain how the same evidence might be used to prove something is true.

What is...?

Abstract reasoning is to work things out using logical thinking.

We all know what we mean when we say that something is true, but to define what we mean by 'truth' is difficult. When we say something is true, we mean that we accept it as right and that there is evidence to support our opinion. The type of evidence that is used to prove something is true can be placed in the categories of scientific, historical, moral and spiritual.

Scientific truth

Many people will only accept the truth of something when it is proved true using scientific evidence. Scientists use observation, **hypothesis**, experiment and repeated testing to prove something true. Scientific truths are **objective** because they are not just one person's opinion. Scientific truth is constantly changing because observation and experiment may result in new evidence that proves earlier scientific theories untrue or inaccurate. Scientific truths are seen to be 'hard' truth because of the evidence used to support them, and for many people the trustworthiest kind.

One of the methods used in science to prove a hypothesis is observation. Through experiment and observation, the truth of a theory is discovered.

Observation alone cannot be relied on to prove scientific truth. For example, the Ancient Greeks observed the movement of the planets and stars and concluded that the earth was at the centre of the universe and all the heavenly bodies revolved around it. They reasoned that as the planets and stars stayed in the heavens rather than falling to earth, it must mean that they were made of a light substance that floated.

In the seventeenth century, Galileo was the first astronomer to use a telescope to observe the planets and stars. Galileo's observations and measurements of the movement of the planets and stars led him to develop the hypothesis that the planets, including the earth, moved around the sun. Observation and experiment by later scientists proved Galileo's hypothesis to be true.

Historical truth

A historian does not need a scientific explanation to accept something is true. Historians use evidence from the time they are researching to support what they believe to be true about that era. This evidence may be based on archaeological finds or historical documents. Some facts about history can be backed up by very firm evidence that all historians can agree on. But a historian has to interpret the evidence to explain *why* things happened so different historians may use the same evidence to reach different conclusions about the era. Such historical truths are **subjective** as there is no proof for this kind of historical question.

Moral truth

When people decide whether an action is right or wrong behaviour, they are making a moral decision. People do not always agree about behaviour that is right and behaviour that is wrong, but what they believe to be right and what they believe to be wrong is described as a moral truth. Moral truth is based on **abstract reasoning**. It is not possible to prove a moral truth by scientific experiment or historical evidence because moral truths are subjective. People do not always agree about what is morally true – what might be right in one circumstance may be considered wrong in another.

Spiritual truth

We have established that scientists use observation and experiment to establish scientific truth and historians use historical evidence to establish historical truth. A moral truth is established by abstract reasoning to decide what is right behaviour in a given situation. There is another form of truth to be considered and this is spiritual truth. Spiritual truth is what a believer claims to be true about the existence of God, the origin of the universe, and the purpose of life. The evidence used to establish spiritual truth, not only involves abstract reasoning but also experience, belief, trust and faith.

When believers make claims about the truth of their religious beliefs, they may use evidence drawn from the religious authorities and sacred writings, their conscience that they might regard as the inner voice of God, religious experience, the history of the religion, scientific theories about the origin of the universe, and from observation of the natural world. Believers use this evidence to reason that their beliefs are true, but the main source of evidence to support the truth of their beliefs is their faith.

Why did the dinosaurs die out?

Activity

1 Read pages 34–5.

2 Write a paragraph to explain the different ways in which people make moral decisions.

3 Explain why moral truth is subjective. Include the use of conscience to make moral decisions in your answer.

Activity

1 List the evidence that a historian might use to prove why the dinosaurs died out.

2 List the evidence that a historian might use to prove that Charles I was beheaded.

3 Why is the truth that Charles I was beheaded objective, whereas a historian's reason for the extinction of the dinosaurs is subjective?

Questions ?

1 'The moon is made of cream cheese.' How might a scientist establish the truth of this statement?

2 'Chocolate was rationed during World War II.' How might a historian establish the truth of this statement?

3 How do people decide what is moral truth?

4 'You can never establish the truth about anything.' Do you agree? Give reasons for your answer, showing that you have thought about more than one point of view.

The nature of spirituality

Activity

1 Read pages 26–9.

2 'There is no evidence that a believer can use to prove a spiritual truth.' Do you agree? Give reasons for your answer, showing that you have thought about more than one point of view. Refer to specific evidence religious believers might use to support their beliefs.

Activity

1 Make notes on the three types of claim to truth used by Christians.

- Religious authority, page 26
- Sacred writings, pages 26–7
- Conscience, page 27.

2 Write an explanation of how each of these three areas make claims to the truth and explain the strengths and weaknesses of each as claims.

What is...?

Spirituality is to be concerned with the mind or spirit rather than the physical body. It may include being concerned with religious matters. It is the opposite of material.

A dance at the Moulin de la Galette, painted by Renoir in 1876

Claims to truth

Religious believers are searching for a meaning in life. They are seeking answers to spiritual questions such as: 'Why are we here?', 'What happens when we die?', and 'How should we live our lives?' These are all spiritual questions that have been answered for believers by the teachings of their faith. Believers accept the answers as spiritual truths that provide the faith with accepted answers but not total understanding of the meaning and purpose of life. The Christian traditions use three main types of claims to truth. These are:

- sacred writings
- religious authorities
- conscience.

Religious believers may have the inner certainty that God exists (faith), but God is never matter-of-fact or simply another material thing in our material world. Christians, for example, recognise that God must always seem a mystery to them as God is outside time and space and beyond human understanding. God is transcendent.

It is very difficult to describe **spirituality**. There are so many different ways in which people feel spiritual and in which spirituality is expressed. Some ways to think about the nature of spirituality include:

- 'the meaning of life'. When people look outside the regular pattern of their lives and think a spiritual thought about life, for example, 'Is there any point to it all?'
- feelings of awe, wonder and mystery. When, for example, an individual looks at the beauty of nature
- inspiration and creativity are linked to spirituality. When, for example, artists are said to have felt inspired by something greater than themselves.

What do you think? ?

'The sun will rise tomorrow.' Think about this statement. Can we state with certainty that this statement is true or only that it is probably true? List the reasons for having certainty about the statement and reasons why the statement is only probably true. Discuss with the rest of the class whether you think that there is anything in life of which we can be certain and possible reasons why there can be certainty.

Activity

The way in which artists express their view of the world through paintings is often regarded as spiritual because they are trying to convey a 'meaning of life' and whether or not there is any point to it all.

1 Look at the two paintings on this spread.

2 What do you think each artist thought was the meaning and purpose of life?

Activity

1 Look back at the section about special revelation on pages 28–9.

2 Write a paragraph to explain the nature of spirituality for a believer who has a special revelation.

The Cry, Edward Munch (1863–1944)

Expressing spirituality

The building of York Minster was regarded as an act of worship in itself

What is...?

An **evangelist** is someone who seeks to spread a religious message to others.

A **missionary** is an evangelist who takes the religious message to people of other countries.

What is...?

Piety is to be devout or religious. It is to show religious devotion.

A **symbol** is a drawing or an object that represents or recalls an idea or belief.

Activity

St Paul was an evangelist and missionary. Use the Internet and/or library to find out about his missionary journeys, especially the many dangers he faced. Discuss with the rest of the class why St Paul was willing to take these risks.

For a Christian, faith means more than simply believing that God exists. It means that they must trust in the love of God and God's support in their lives. In return, Christians believe that they must show love of God by a commitment to a specific lifestyle.

Most Christians feel the need to express their spirituality in society. There are three main ways through which Christians do this:

- individual commitment to the faith
- belonging to a faith community
- supporting voluntary organisations.

Individual commitment

Some believers are inspired to express their feelings about God creatively through literature, art or music. For others, it may be the design of their place of worship. The size and design of medieval cathedrals is an example of how awe and wonder is expressed through the design of a building. For others, their faith leads them to a desire to share their beliefs with others as an **evangelist** or **missionary**.

Christians hope to draw closer to God through acts of worship. These acts of **piety** may be in private or in public. Some Christians will withdraw from everyday life for a time to give their full attention to God and Jesus. This is called 'going on retreat'. Other Christians may believe that they have spiritual calling (a vocation). This could be to leave their daily lives and become a monk or nun so that they can spend much of each day seeking to get closer to God without the distractions of daily life. Other people's vocation might be to serve God by working in a profession as a teacher, nurse or doctor. For others, their vocation might be to work with people who are underprivileged in some way such as the homeless.

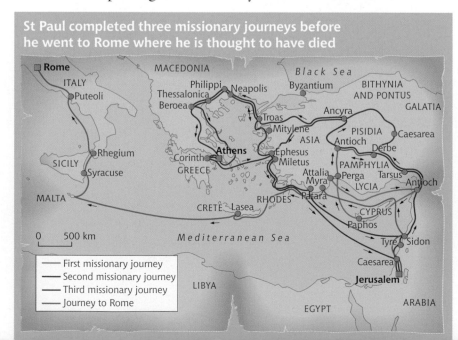

St Paul completed three missionary journeys before he went to Rome where he is thought to have died

Most Christians express their spirituality through private prayer or by studying the Bible. Most Christians believe that the Bible is the Word of God and it is used in most forms of Christian worship. However, the focus given to the Bible in worship varies from tradition to tradition. In most Protestant Churches the Bible is the main focus of worship and it is believed that salvation can be achieved by living by the truths contained in the Bible. Catholics, members of the Church of England, and Orthodox Christians, believe that the way to salvation is through the consecrated bread and wine of Holy Communion.

Symbolism plays an important part in the worship of many Christians, as the **symbols** used remind them of an aspect of Christian belief and helps them to concentrate on God and Jesus.

Faith communities

Most Christians meet with other Christians who share their beliefs for an act of public (corporate) worship. Most Christians value being part of a faith community because it has many benefits for them. These benefits include:

- the strengthening of an individual's faith by worshipping alongside others who share their beliefs
- an opportunity to make a public witness of their faith
- feeling that the act of worship brings them closer to God
- pastoral support from other members of the community, particularly the leader
- greater understanding of the faith and how to live according to the teachings of the faith is gained by discussing aspects of the faith with other members of the community
- opportunities to provide service to others, possibly through acts of charity.

Corporate worship in Christianity takes many forms. The form of Christian worship depends on the tradition to which the Christian belongs. For example, both Catholics and Quakers (The Society of Friends) believe that Christ is present during their worship but the form of the worship is very different.

Voluntary organisations

Another way by which a religious believer shows commitment to their faith and express their spirituality in society is to help others. Christians may give up time for voluntary work or to raise money for a good cause. Christians may support secular (non-religious) organisations or specific Christian organisations.

Activity

1 Using the Internet and/or library, find out how the following aids to prayer are used by Christians as an expression of individual commitment to the faith:

- the rosary as an aid to Catholic prayer
- icons as an aid to Orthodox prayer
- the cross
- the crucifix.

2 Write a paragraph to explain how each symbol acts as an aid to private worship.

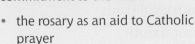

Activity

The class is to divide into groups of four or five people. Each group must choose one of the secular voluntary organisations from the list below.

- Amnesty International UK
- Barnardo's
- Greenpeace
- Help the Aged
- Oxfam International
- National Society for the Prevention of Cruelty to Children (NSPCC)
- The Samaritans
- Voluntary Service Overseas (VSO).

Using the Internet and/or the library, the group is to research the work of the organisation, including how funds are raised to support the work of the organisation. Each group's research is to provide the basis of a presentation about the work of the organisation to the rest of the class.

the nature of truth and spirituality?

Task 1

1 Explain in your own words what is meant by:
 - scientific truth
 - historical truth
 - moral truth
 - spiritual truth.

2 For each of the types of truth you have explained, give examples of the evidence that would be used to prove each of the different types of truth.

3 'The only type of truth that can be proved with certainty is scientific truth.' Do you agree? Give reasons for your answer, showing that you have thought about more than one point of view. Refer to religious teaching in your answer.

Task 2

1 What is meant by 'spirituality'?

2 'Spontaneous worship is more spiritual than worship that follows a set pattern.' Do you agree? Give reasons for your answer, showing that you have thought about more than one point of view. Refer to specific Christian worship in your answer.

Task 3

Below are descriptions of a Quaker meeting and a Catholic Mass. They are two different ways by which Christians express spirituality in public worship.

1 Read the description of the Quaker meeting.

2 Read the description of the Catholic Mass.

3 Explain how the form of worship in each of the Christian traditions are different.

4 Explain the reasons for any similarities between the two forms of Christian worship.

5 'The use of symbolic actions and hymn-singing makes it easier for Christians to express their spirituality rather than sitting in silent mediation.' Do you agree? Give reasons for your answer, showing that you have thought about more than one point of view. Refer to specific features of Catholic and Quaker worship in your answer.

Quakers (The Society of Friends)

Quakers do not celebrate Holy Communion. They believe that communion with God is an inward grace brought through the gift of the Holy Spirit and no outward action is needed.

Quaker worship is very different from the Catholic Mass

Quakers have no formal services and the services do not include hymn-singing. Quakers sit quietly meditating until someone feels moved by the Holy Spirit to speak. When a Quaker stands to speak this is called a ministry. A meeting could last for an hour without anyone speaking or several people may speak and share their thoughts with the meeting. Someone might say a prayer or read a section of the Bible or a poem. At the end of the hour, one of the leaders of the group will bring the service to a close by shaking hands with the person on each side of them. At the end of the service notices are read.

The Catholic Mass

The Catholic Church teaches that the Mass (Holy Communion) is the most important act of worship. There are important features to a Mass to remind the believers that Christ's sacrifice for the forgiveness of sins is repeated at

The priest consecrates the bread and wine on the altar

each service. Catholics believe the bread and wine are believed to be food and drink for the spiritual life of the communicants (that is, those taking part in the Mass) to gain eternal life and God's forgiveness.

Catholics believe that only an ordained priest may bless the bread and wine. When the priest dedicates (consecrates) the bread and wine through the action of the Holy Spirit, the bread and wine become the actual body and blood of Christ. This is called transubstantiation. Catholics believe that Christ is present and his sacrifice is repeated at each Mass. Christ's presence means the congregation must show respect and this involves bowing from the knee and the use of incense. Throughout the service, the congregation will make set responses to the words used by the priest.

The service begins with the priest greeting the people and praying to God to forgive sins. The reading of bible passages and a sermon follows. A statement of belief called the Nicene Creed and five prayers for the faithful are said.

The most important part of the service now takes place. The bread, wine, and collections are brought to the altar. The bread is placed on a dish called a paten. The wine is held in a cup called a chalice. The priest prays that the gifts are acceptable to God and swings the incense over them. The priest washes his hands and the congregation prays. The priest thanks and praises God and asks the Holy Spirit to make the bread and wine holy. A bell rings to welcome the Holy Spirit. The priest spreads his hands over them and as he prays he uses the words of Jesus at the Last Supper. The priest consecrates the bread and wine. As he does this, he lifts the bread and then the wine for the congregation to see. The bread and wine are now called the Host and the raising of the bread and wine by the priest is called the Elevation of the Host. As this happens, a bell is rung three times. This is the moment when transubstantiation takes place. The congregation shows adoration in silence. The priest reminds them of the meaning of Christ's sacrifice for their sins and that by taking communion the congregation share in this sacrifice. There are further prayers and the sign of peace is offered when the congregation shake hands with each other.

The bread used in the Catholic Church is called the wafer. The priest holds up a wafer and breaks it in half to symbolise how Christ's body was broken on the cross. The priest will now eat the wafer and drink the wine. The congregation come forward and stand in line to receive the wafer, which the priest places on their tongue, saying, 'The body of Christ'. If the wine is given, he says, 'The blood of Christ'.

The service ends with a blessing from the priest and the words, 'The Mass is ended. Go in peace to love and serve the Lord.' Catholics are being reminded that because of Jesus' sacrifice for their sins, part of their duty as a believer is to work for others.

Task 4

1 Why do you think Mother Teresa chose to enter a convent?

2 Why do you think she also devoted her life to the care of the dying?

3 Using the Internet and/or the library, research the life and work of a Christian religious community. Write a detailed description of how life in the community seeks to develop the spirituality of a monk or nun.

Mother Teresa combined the spiritual life of a nun with helping the dying on the streets of Calcutta

Citizenship Link

Imagine that you are a local reporter writing a story about the work of a local voluntary group. Choose a local voluntary group and find out how the group helps the local community. You could attend one of the group's meetings and/or interview members of the group. Having completed your research, write the newspaper article. Remember to include in your article any social changes that the group has brought about in the area.

God and life

Christians believe in the sanctity of life because they believe that God creates all human beings as individuals with the right to life. Christian beliefs about God as creator include the belief that all human beings are created as individuals. Every individual is unique and unlike any other individual in the universe. God is responsible for each life and decided each person's identity before he or she was born. Human beings have a special place in God's eyes and in God's creation.

Christians agree that God is the creator of life but disagree at which stage in the pregnancy life begins.

Catholics believe that life begins at the moment of conception when the sperm fertilises the ovum (egg).

The Church of England teaches that life begins at about fourteen days when the first anatomical feature, the primitive streak, appears. Prior to this point, the embryo can split into more than one individual and therefore the Church argues that up to that point, the embryo cannot be a distinct human being.

Is this the moment at which life begins?

Other Christians have different views about when life begins. The stages at which some Christians believe that life begins include:

- the moment of implantation when the fertilised egg (blastocyst) becomes attached to the mother's womb
- when the embryo's heart begins to beat or movement first takes place
- at the moment of birth when the child takes his or her first independent breath.

Human fertilisation

There are many conditions that cause men and women to be infertile. For example, a woman with blocked fallopian tubes does not release fertile eggs into the womb to be fertilised by her male partner's sperm. A man with a low sperm count has a limited chance of fathering a child. In the past the only hope for a couple that could not conceive a child was adoption. However, genetic engineering has given biologists a greater understanding of the origins of life. It has become possible to create life outside the

Activity

Read Psalm 139:13, 15 on page 46.

In Psalm 138:13, 15 it suggests that God created every part of a human being and that God knows the identity of each person before they are born. How might a Christian use this passage to support their view of when they believe that life begins?

Activity

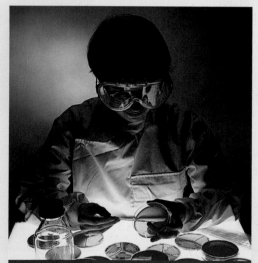

In IVF, the eggs and sperm taken from a couple are fertilised in a glass dish

Use the Internet, newspapers and television programmes to find out the most recent developments in human fertilisation.

womb. Since the first 'test-tube' baby, Louise Brown, born in 1978, there have been significant developments in fertility treatment.

These include:

- *in vitro* fertilisation (IVF), when the ovum is fertilised in a 'test tube' and then implanted in the woman's womb. The ovum may be the woman's or donated by another woman. The ovum is then fertilised by the semen of the woman's husband. If both partners are infertile then the embryo implanted may be donated. Embryos can now be produced by IVF and frozen until a woman wishes to have a baby.

- AID (artificial insemination by donor), when the mother's egg is artificially inseminated with a donor's sperm because her male partner is infertile.

- AIH (artificial insemination by husband), when the husband's sperm is artificially placed into the woman.

- surrogacy, when a woman bears the child for a woman who cannot become pregnant. The woman may become pregnant through the implantation of a fertilised egg from the couple seeking to have a child or from donated sperm or egg. When the child is born, the woman hands the child over.

Surrogacy is when a woman bears the child for a woman who cannot become pregnant

The Human Fertilisation and Embryology Act 1990 regulates on IVF. It also sets out the conditions for surrogacy, including the right of the surrogate mother not to have to give up the baby. The couple arranging the surrogacy have to be married, over eighteen, and have to provide either the sperm or ovum of the surrogate. Under the Surrogacy Arrangement Act 1985, it makes it an offence to advertise surrogacy services or for a company or agency to be paid for arranging the surrogacy. The surrogate mother cannot be paid for the baby and may only claim any medical expenses she incurs.

Activity

1 Using the Internet and/or library, find out about Childlessness Overcome Through Surrogacy (COTS).

2 Write an account of their work and views on surrogacy.

What do you think? ?

1 How do you think you would feel if you suddenly discovered that you were a test-tube baby?
2 Do you think that all children have the right to know the details of their biological parents?

Questions

1 How might Christians apply the idea of the sanctity of life to arguments about the right and wrong use of *in vitro* fertilisation?
2 Explain different Christian understandings of when life begins.
3 Explain what is meant by artificial insemination and surrogacy.

Fertility treatment

What is...?

Embryology is the study of embryos.

Genetics is the science that studies all aspects of inherited characteristics.

Christians believe that children are a gift from God

Although Christians believe that children are a gift from God and one of the purposes of marriage is reproduction, not all Christians agree with fertility treatment for childless couples. Some Christians believe that it is against the will of God to use artificial insemination. These Christians believe a couple should leave the decision as to whether or not they have children to God.

The Catholic Church teaches that children should only be conceived from natural intercourse within marriage. Any other method goes against God's will. Pope Pius XII condemned AID and surrogacy because 'a third person becoming involved in a marriage is like "mechanical adultery"'. It would therefore be breaking the seventh commandment: 'Do not commit adultery.' The Church allows IVF and AIH under the following conditions:

- no 'spare' embryos are produced
- the sperm and the egg belong to the married couple
- IVF and AIH are not used instead of sexual intercourse between the husband and wife.

It is very difficult to perform infertility treatment without the production of 'spare' embryos so it is very difficult to meet the Catholic Church's criteria for the use of IVF. The Church of England allows the use of IVF so long as it only involves a married couple and 'the treatment should normally be given to women during years, when under normal circumstances, they might conceive' (General Synod, 1997). The Church of England is against surrogacy as it teaches that it is wrong to pay a woman to bear a child for another.

Most Protestants accept AIH and IVF so long as it only involves a married couple and there is no third person involved as they share the Catholic view that this could be classed as 'adultery'.

Embryology and cloning

Embryology is the study of embryos and is an important part of **genetic** engineering. Under the Human Fertilisation and Embryology Act 1990, scientists can use human embryos up until the embryos are fourteen days old. The scientists have to be licensed for research into fertility, contraception, miscarriages, congenital diseases, and chromosome abnormalities. The law does not allow the use of embryos for research into diseases. In February 2002, British scientists were allowed the use of embryonic stem cells as a source of spare body tissue for transplants and the cloning of embryos for medical research.

Cloning is the process of making a genetically identical animal, plant or human without the normal sexual reproduction process.

This means that the cloned organism is created using DNA from a single parent. No sperm is used in cloning. The nucleus of the egg, which contains the DNA, is extracted and replaced with the nucleus of an adult cell. It then begins to divide like a normal fertilised egg.

The cloning of Dolly the Sheep has raised the possibility that humans could be cloned. Advances in science means that scientists have now cloned cats, sheep, cows, pigs, mice and goats, and are working on horses. However, many cloned animals have developed severe abnormalities. This has raised concerns about the cloning of humans. Parliament has approved the cloning of humans for medical research so long as they are not allowed to develop beyond the embryo stage. There is a ban on the birth of human clones.

Dolly the Sheep was the first cloned mammal (1996)

Most Christians are not against animal cloning as long as the animals are cared for and treated with respect. This is because the cloning of animals could help to solve the problems of hunger in the developing world. However, most Christians believe that each person has a special relationship with God, is created as an individual, and are opposed to the cloning of human beings. These Christians believe cloning goes against the sanctity of life.

Many Christians are concerned that embryos could become a financial commodity, bought and sold for experimental use. They feel that this would be exploitation and against God's teaching.

Some Christians believe that the work of the genetic engineers may be going against God's plan for the world and fear that scientists are seeking to put themselves in the place of God. Other Christians argue that as God made us in 'his image', God has given us the ability to learn and develop. Genetic engineering may be part of God's plan for human development. There is no direct teaching in the Bible about the new science of embryology: Christians have to apply relevant biblical teaching to the sanctity of life and the right of humans to control life.

The Catholic Church believes life begins at the moment of conception and embryos are human beings made in the image of God and possessing a soul. The Catholic Church teaches that the use of embryos in embryology is a sin as it is breaking the commandment, 'Do not murder'.

The Church of England is against the production of human embryos specifically for research and does not believe any human embryos should be used after they are fourteen days old.

Quakers have not produced a statement about embryology but believe that considerable thought should be given to how far scientists should go with their research.

Questions ?

1 How might Christian teachings and beliefs about when life begins influence a Christian's decision about fertility treatment?

2 Choose **two** different Christian traditions and outline the teachings of each about fertility treatment.

3 'IVF is playing God.' Do you agree? Give reasons for your answer, showing that you have thought about more than one point of view.

Tasks on 'Religious attitudes to … matters of life' can be found at the end of the following unit, 'Religious attitudes to … matters of death' (Unit 12)

When does life end?

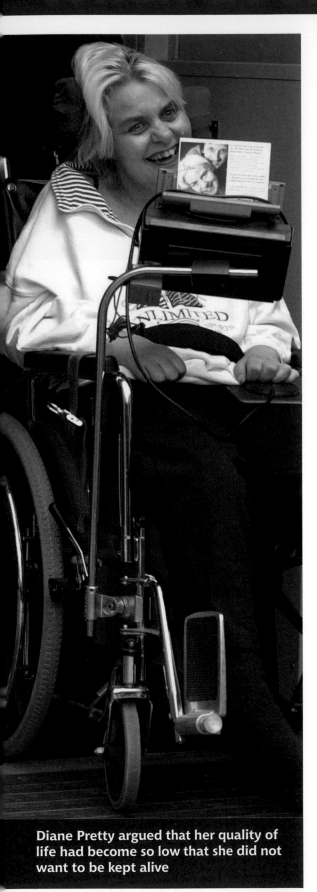

Diane Pretty argued that her quality of life had become so low that she did not want to be kept alive

The belief in the sanctity of life means that Christians have to decide not only when life begins but also when life ends. In the past people were declared dead when their heart stopped beating. However, advances in medical science have meant that it is possible to keep a person's heart beating by machine and so a new definition of death was introduced. A person is now declared 'brain dead' when there is no response to any form of stimulus.

The advances in medical science have left some people alive but with a quality of life that many people regard as no life at all. For example, there are people who are in what is called a 'persistant vegetative state' (PVS). These people are able to breathe for themselves but have no awareness of their identity or their surroundings. They have to be artificially fed. There are other people who are kept alive by machine and if the machine failed then they would die. People question whether such people are truly alive.

An individual's views on when life ends might be affected by their beliefs about life after death. Christians believe that death is only the continuation of an eternal life. Many Christians believe that this is with God for those who have accepted Christ. In the Apostles' Creed, Christians state that they believe that after death there will be the 'resurrection of the body', and 'life everlasting'. Most Christians are comforted by knowing that when loved ones die, they are with God in heaven and that all their suffering in this world is ended.

Most Christians believe that God judges them on their actions in life and they must avoid any action that might result in God's punishment. Some Christian traditions, for example, the Calvinists, believe that God has already decided who will go to heaven and who will not. Most Christian traditions, however, say that God will forgive sins and it is up to peoples' actions and beliefs as to whether they go to heaven or not. Jesus taught that people would be judged on how they have helped those in need, including the sick. When they see someone suffering through illness, Christians have to decide whether help should include ending that suffering through death or trying to reduce that suffering through the care they give.

What do you think? ?

Look back to the explanation of sanctity of life and quality of life on pages 40–1. How do you think a believer may apply each of these terms to when life ends?

Euthanasia

Euthanasia is the practice of ending the life of people who are suffering from incurable diseases or handicap, using painless methods. The intention of euthanasia is to avoid prolonging their suffering. It is sometimes called mercy killing. Voluntary euthanasia occurs when a person requests death to end their suffering and is helped to die. It is legal in some countries, like the Netherlands. Strict regulations control its use. Euthanasia is illegal in the UK.

Involuntary euthanasia occurs when the person has no part in the decision-making process to end their suffering. This may be because the patient is in a persistent vegetative state. UK courts do sometimes allow doctors to stop feeding patients in a persistent vegetative state if there is no hope of a cure.

Passive euthanasia occurs when no action is taken to prolong life but there is no deliberate action to end the life. For example, if a person dying of cancer has a heart attack, there would be no attempt to resuscitate him or her. Active euthanasia is when a deliberate action is taken to end a life, such as the administration of a lethal injection of an overdose of a drug, or the active withdrawal of a life-supporting drug or machine. Some people consider active euthanasia to be assisted **suicide**.

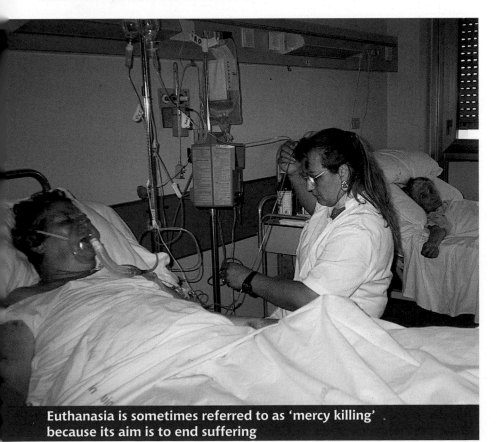

Euthanasia is sometimes referred to as 'mercy killing' because its aim is to end suffering

What is...?

Suicide is taking one's own life.

Activity

Using the Internet and/or library, find out about a case study in which there has been a court case in which a terminally ill patient was seeking euthanasia.

Write a paragraph to explain his or her reasons for wanting euthanasia and the decision the court gave them.

Questions ?

1 Explain different Christian views about life after death.
2 What is euthanasia?
3 Explain the difference between passive euthanasia and active euthanasia.
4 Explain the difference between voluntary euthanasia and involuntary euthanasia.
5 Why have some people felt that it is a person's ultimate right to decide how they want to die?

Most Christians believe that God is the giver of life and it is up to God to make the decision when a life ends.

Some Christians argue that people have a choice between life and death and that God is instructing them to choose life so they argue that euthanasia is a sin. Other Christians believe that people who are suffering should have the right to die with dignity, and God has given people freedom to choose to live or die.

Some Christians accept passive euthanasia, as it is not furthering a person's suffering and it is placing the choice as to whether the person lives or dies in God's hands. They accept that the painkillers given to ease the suffering of terminally ill patients hastens death, but do not regard it as a deliberate action to kill the person. Christians who support passive euthanasia may oppose active euthanasia because it is a deliberate action to end a person's life. They regard active euthanasia as murder and believe that it breaks the sixth commandment, 'Do not commit murder.'

Other Christians do support active euthanasia. These Christians might argue that when God made humans in 'his image', he gave people intelligence and the freedom to make choices about their life, including when they want to die, especially as they believe that God would not want people to suffer when their suffering might be ended.

Arguments for euthanasia

- People should be allowed to decide for themselves when they want to die. Suicide is legal so why not euthanasia?

- Life comes from God, but there is nothing in the Bible that states that a person must be kept alive at any cost. It is wrong to artificially preserve life beyond its natural span and this may be going against God's plan: 'He sets the time for birth and the time for death, … the time for killing and the time for healing.' (Ecclesiastes 3:1–3)

- Keeping people alive by machine or in a permanent vegetative state is not life in the true sense. Jesus said: 'I have come in order that you might have life – life in all its fullness' (John 10:10), and so some Christians argue that if this is not possible then people have the right to die.

- Euthanasia allows people to die with dignity. The person can die with their family and friends around them in a loving atmosphere, with all their affairs in order.

- Relatives would be spared the risk of watching loved ones suffer a slow, painful death.

Activity

When making moral decisions related to issues such as euthanasia, Christians consider not only the sanctity of life but also the quality of life. Look back to pages 40–1.

How do Christians measure an individual's quality of life and how might this affect a Christian's attitude towards euthanasia?

'I am now giving you the choice between life and death, between God's blessing and God's curse, and I call heaven and earth to witness the choice you make. Choose life.' (Deuteronomy 30:19)

- Animals are not allowed to suffer and the same compassion should be shown to humans.

Arguments against euthanasia

The Catholic Church and many other Christians are against euthanasia.

- Euthanasia is always wrong because if it is involuntary euthanasia, it is murder, and if the person does request euthanasia, it is suicide. Both of which the Church regards as sins. Euthanasia breaks the sixth commandment, 'Do not commit murder.' (Exodus 20:12)

- God is the giver of life and therefore only God may end it. God has fixed how long a person will live and euthanasia goes against God's plan.

From one human being he created all races on earth and made them live throughout the whole earth. He himself fixed beforehand the exact times and the limits of the places where they would live. (Acts 17:26)

- St Paul taught that because Jesus died to save the world from sin then people cannot do as they wish: 'You do not belong to yourselves but to God' (1 Corinthians 6:19). 'If we live, we are responsible to the Lord, and when we die we are responsible to the Lord. Both in life and in death we belong to the Lord.' (Romans 14:18)

- It is not for an individual to try to escape from God's plan that we cannot know. God may have plans for people even when it appears that their life is finished. The physicist, Stephen Hawking has motor neuron disease. He was not expected to live long when he was first diagnosed with the disease. But since he became paralysed, he has achieved great things in his career, made important scientific discoveries and written best-selling books.

- St Paul taught that the human body is a 'temple to God' and it is wrong to destroy God's temple:

Surely you know that you are God's temple and that God's Spirit lives in you! So if anyone destroys God's temple, God will destroy him. For God's temple is holy, and you yourselves are his temple.' (1 Corinthians 3:16–17)

- Helping the sick, disabled and elderly, teaches compassion. It offers the chance to put Christian teaching into practise.

Some Christians believe that euthanasia shows a lack of faith in God. God may send a miracle to cure them.

Activity

Read the Parable of the Sheep and the Goats on page 77. Write a paragraph to explain how this parable might be applied to the care of the terminally ill.

Questions ?

1 Why do some Christians accept passive euthanasia but are against active euthanasia?
2 Explain **four** reasons why some Christians oppose euthanasia.
3 Explain **four** reasons why some Christians might support euthanasia.

Death and care

Dame Cicely Saunders founded the Hospice Movement

The Hospice Movement

Many Christians believe that the reason why people request euthanasia is because they are afraid of the pain or loss of dignity that might result from a terminal illness. The provision of the correct care for the dying can give them dignity and freedom from pain and the result is the patient no longer seeks euthanasia. This is the aim of hospices. The Hospice Movement provides surroundings in which a dying person's emotional and spiritual needs are met as well as the physical ones.

A hospice is a special type of hospital or home that cares for terminally ill patients. The care that they are given is not only to reduce their pain but also to address any worries that they may have about dying.

Suicide

Many people regard voluntary euthanasia as assisted suicide. Many Christians believe that although the law of Britain allows people to take their life, suicide is not what God wants. Life is a gift from God and however difficult life becomes it is not for people to decide to end it. They support their view with Acts 17:26 because it states that God has fixed our lifespan and suicide would be against God's plan. Many Christians believe that it shows a lack of faith and trust in God's good purpose. St Paul taught that God would give no more suffering than people can cope with and they must accept what happens.

Quakers believe that 'every stage of our lives offers fresh opportunities' and whatever happens in life people should learn from it. If, however, someone commits suicide, Quakers do not believe that they have the right to condemn them. Many Christians now share this view. Most will seek to do everything possible to help a person considering taking their own life. Some Christians support the work of the Samaritans, as they believe that if people have someone to talk to, there is less risk of them taking their own life.

Care of the sick and the elderly

Many sick, elderly and disabled people have felt suicidal because they feel alone or a burden to their family or society. Many Christians believe that if people are given the right care then they will not want to die.

One function of the family is to meet the human needs of love and companionship. The family provides an economic unit in which everyone is supported, including the sick, disabled and the elderly.

The Reverend Chad Varah established the Samaritans

The nuclear family is usually one or two adults living with their own or adopted children. The extended family includes grandparents, aunts and uncles, as well as nephews, nieces and cousins. In many societies the extended family live together and take the shared responsibility of bringing up the children, caring for the sick and elderly members of the family, and sharing expenses. There is always someone to turn to when things go wrong as well as sharing all the family celebrations.

In modern Britain, employment causes many people to move away from their family and so the family support is no longer available. The result is that many sick, disabled and elderly people have to depend on the local authorities rather than their families for care. They may be provided with carers to visit them in their homes or placed in sheltered accommodation or residential homes.

Most Christians believe that the teaching of Jesus makes it clear that they have a duty to help the sick, disabled and elderly, and support the work of charities trying to improve such people's quality of life. Christians believe that they have a duty to care for the elderly as God commands them to 'Respect your father and your mother' (Exodus 20:12). Many churches collect food at their harvest festival service for the elderly as well as organising social events for them.

Activity

Using the Internet and/or library, research the life and work of Dame Cicely Saunders.

Activity

Using the Internet and/or library, research the work of the Samaritans.

Design a leaflet that could be distributed to people contemplating suicide to explain how the Samaritans could help.

Questions ?

1 How do hospices seek to overcome the problems facing the terminally ill?

2 What is suicide?

3 Why are most Christians concerned about suicide?

4 What are the main functions of the family?

5 (a) What is a nuclear family?
  (b) What is an extended family?

6 What differences will there be between a trained nurse caring for an elderly man and a loving daughter caring for her aged father? Give reasons for your answer.

7 Why do you think Christians feel they must help families to overcome their problems? Support your answer with examples of problems which Christians might help families to overcome.

Do you understand …

about religious attitudes to matters of life and death?

Task 1

Read the following passage and answer the questions that follow.

Blood transfusions and transplants

Transplant surgery saves or improves the lives of thousands of people each year. Transplant surgery involves damaged organs, such as kidneys, hearts, lungs, and livers, being replaced by healthy ones from a donor. Some organs such as a heart can only be donated after the death of the donor. Blood transfusions are another way by which people choose to help the sick or injured. Some people attend blood transfusion units to donate blood.

Many Christians choose to make blood and organ donations, even if the organs are transplanted after their death. This is because blood transfusions and the transplant of organs seek to preserve life. They are regarded as ways of helping the sick and in the Parable of the Sheep and the Goats Jesus praised people who helped the sick. In the parable Jesus warns people that they will be judged on how well they have followed his teaching to help people in need. Jesus lists people who should be helped:

'I was hungry and you fed me, thirsty and you gave me a drink; I was a stranger and you received me in your homes, naked and you clothed me; I was sick and you took care of me, in prison and you visited me.' (Matthew 25:35–6)

Jesus states that those who have helped such people will be rewarded and those who have ignored those in need will be punished.

1 Explain the term 'transplant surgery'.

2 What is a blood transfusion?

3 Why do some Christians apply the Parable of the Sheep and the Goats to organ donation and blood transfusions?

4 Why do you think that Christians who reject cloning are happy to give blood or to carry an organ donor card?

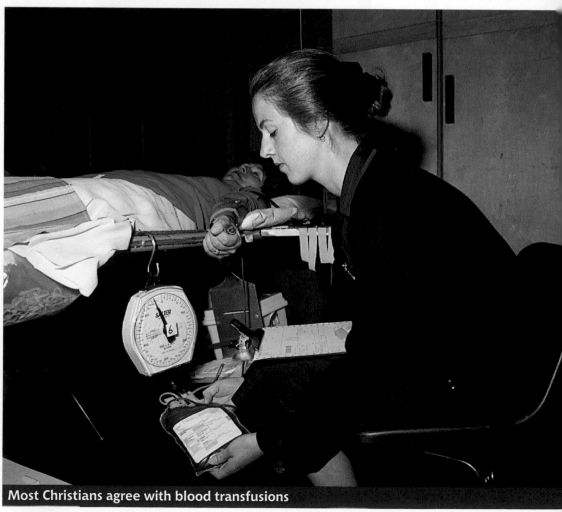

Most Christians agree with blood transfusions

Task 2

1 Explain what is meant by '*in vitro* fertilisation' and why is it used?

2 How might religious teachings and beliefs influence a Christian's decision about *in vitro* fertilisation? Refer to religious teaching in your answer.

Task 3

'Life begins at the moment of conception so embryology is wrong.' Do you agree? Give reasons for your answer, showing that you have thought about more than one point of view. Refer to religious teaching in your answer.

Task 4

'And to love God with all your heart and with all your mind and with all your strength, and to love your neighbour as yourself, is more important than to offer animals and other sacrifices to God.' (Mark 12:33)

1 What two commandments did Jesus give to people?

2 How might the teaching in Mark 12:33 be applied to medical research?

Task 5

1 Explain the work of a hospice.

2 Explain the different attitudes of Christians to euthanasia. Support your answer with the influence of religious teachings and beliefs.

3 'It's my life so I should have the right to end it.' Do you agree? Give reasons for your answer, showing that you have thought about more than one point of view. Refer to religious teaching in your answer.

You created me, and you keep me safe (Psalm 119:73)

Citizenship Link

Using the Internet, newspapers and television programmes, research human cloning. Write a report for your teacher on the current developments in human cloning. Include in your report reasons for and against the cloning of humans.

Drug abuse 1

Why do people take drugs?

There are many reasons people give for taking **drugs**. The reasons include the following.

- It makes them feel good or better. Many people claim not to be able to start the day without a cup of coffee, for example.

- People claim that they feel more relaxed if they have a drink of alcohol or smoke a cigarette, especially in social situations.

- Alcohol and nicotine help people to cope with the pressures of life, especially their job. Some people have taken stimulant drugs to help them work longer hours.

- Many people claim to have started taking drugs to be one of the group: peer-pressure.

- Addiction causes people to smoke, drink alcohol or to take drugs, although they would like to give up.

- Some competitors in a sporting event use performance enhancing drugs. Any drugs that might have improved their performance and given them an unfair advantage are banned by the international governing bodies of sport. There are often random tests for performance enhancing drugs and if the tests are proved positive then the person will be banned from competitions for a set time.

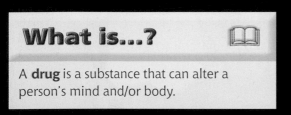

What is...? 📖

A **drug** is a substance that can alter a person's mind and/or body.

Coffee contains the drug caffeine

Legal drugs

Coffee, tea, cola-flavoured drinks and chocolate contain the drug caffeine. Caffeine is a stimulant that makes a person feel more energetic and is addictive. There are no laws against the purchase of products containing caffeine because it is unlikely to kill or cause permanent damage to a person's mind or body.

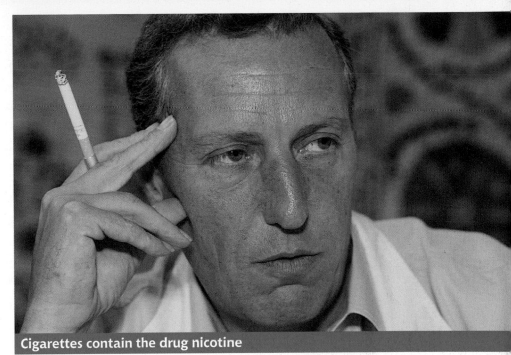

Nicotine is the addictive drug found in tobacco. A smoker's brain quickly starts to rely on it in order to stay clam and carry on a regular life. People also get into the habit of smoking and the habit becomes hard to break. It is illegal to buy tobacco in Britain under the age of sixteen years. Cigarettes carry a health

Cigarettes contain the drug nicotine

warning because it is known that tobacco is a cause of lung cancer and heart disease as well as other respiratory problems. Every year the treatment of smoking-related illnesses costs the National Health Service over £400 million.

Alcohol is a drug in itself. Alcohol cannot be legally purchased by anyone less than eighteen years of age. Although alcohol appears to be a stimulant, it is in fact a depressive drug. This is why people under the influence of alcohol are often violent or commit suicide. Alcohol misuse contributes significantly to crime levels through alcohol specific offences, for example, being drunk and disorderly in public. It has been estimated that 40 per cent of violent crime, 78 per cent of assaults and 88 per cent of criminal damage cases are committed while the offender is under the influence of alcohol.

Excessive drinking of alcohol can damage the brain and liver as well as cause heart disease, strokes and cancer. One in seven road deaths are the result of drink driving. Alcoholics are addicted to alcohol and find that the compulsion to drink often ruins not only their health but also their life.

Some of the revenue raised from taxation on the sales of tobacco and alcohol is used to support medical research and the National Health Service, but many people argue that the cost of the treatment of people for their use of these two drugs is greater than the money raised.

Activity

Using the Internet and/or library, research the work of Alcoholics Anonymous.

List the twelve steps of Alcoholics Anonymous.

Questions

1 What is a drug?
2 **(a)** What are performing enhancing drugs?
   (b) Why would most Christians consider the use of such drugs wrong?
3 Why are there concerns about the use of alcohol and nicotine?

Drug abuse 2

A person found in possession of drugs may be sent to prison

Activity

Find out the current debates related to the legalisation of drugs and write a report on your findings.

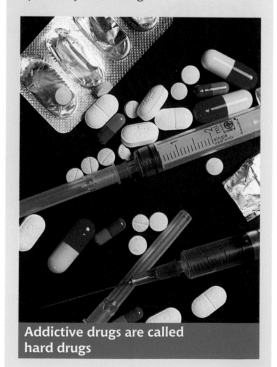

Addictive drugs are called hard drugs

Illegal drugs

Doctors legally prescribe certain drugs to cure an illness or to relieve pain. If these drugs are obtained without prescription then their use is illegal. The illegal drugs are classified according to how dangerous they are. Class A drugs are the most dangerous and their possession carries the greatest penalty under the law.

Class A drugs include: heroin, cocaine and crack cocaine, Ecstasy and LSD (acid).

- All produce a mental high. LSD produces hallucinations.

- All have strong physical effects. Cocaine and LSD increase blood pressure and heart rate and users often experience disorientation, as do Ecstasy users. Heroin often produces constipation and appetite loss.

- All carry serious health risks. Heroin and cocaine (especially crack cocaine) are highly addictive and overdosing is often fatal. Ecstasy has been linked to deaths through overheating (dehydration) and damage to the brain, liver and kidneys. LSD can cause coma and convulsions, and LSD and heroin use can both lead to mental health problems.

- Possession of Class A drugs carries a maximum punishment of seven years in prison and/or a heavy fine. Supplying them can mean life imprisonment and/or a heavy fine.

Class B drugs include amphetamines.

- Amphetamines produce a 'rush', a feeling of increased energy and speed. The effects of amphetamine use include increased heart rate, tiredness and depression after use. High doses of amphetamines cause panic attacks and hallucinations. Long-term use can cause mental illness and heart problems.

- Possession of Class B drugs carries a maximum penalty of five years in prison and/or a fine. Supplying them can result in fourteen years in prison and/or a fine.

In July 2002, the UK government proposed that cannabis be changed from a Class B to a Class C drug. This does not mean it has become legal. Class C drugs include cannabis, tranquillisers and anabolic steroids, which are usually taken in tablet form to enhance sporting performance.

- Tranquillisers have a calming effect and reduce anxiety. Anabolic steroids enable people to train harder, build muscle faster, and are used by athletes.

- Tranquillisers can affect memory; anabolic steroids can produce feelings of aggression.

- The health risks of tranquillisers are that they can be addictive and are very dangerous when mixed with alcohol. With anabolic steroids women may develop more facial hair, deeper voice, and there is also a risk of miscarriage. Men may develop impotence and sterility and there are heart and liver risks, too.

- The maximum penalty for possession of cannabis is two years in prison and/or a fine. For supplying cannabis, the maximum penalty is five years in prison and/or a fine. For anabolic steroids and tranquillisers, possession is not illegal but supply is.

- As performance enhancing drugs have been banned in sport, athletes will be tested for anabolic steroids before major competitions. A positive test will disqualify an athlete from a sport, often for many years.

Drugs are often classed as being 'hard' or 'soft' according to their addictive properties.

Hard drugs are Class A drugs and they are addictive drugs. These drugs not only lead to ill health or even the death of addicts, but also cause many addicts to commit crimes to get the money they need to support their habit. The problems associated with the illegal use of hard drugs have led to people considering their legalisation. However, the health risks from hard drugs are so high that many others oppose legalisation.

Drugs that are not physically addictive are called soft drugs. Cannabis is the soft drug that produces a mental high and feeling of relaxation, and of being more sociable. It causes the most debate and some people want it to be legalised.

Arguments for legalising cannabis include:

- Cannabis is not physically addictive and is less harmful than alcohol, which is legal.

- Cannabis is helpful in relieving the suffering of people with illnesses like multiple sclerosis.

- Legalising cannabis would free up police to deal with more serious offences.

Arguments against legalising cannabis include:

- The long-term effects of taking cannabis could be harmful and are not as yet known but have been linked to the same health problems as suffered by smokers, including lung cancer.

- Cannabis can cause dangerous driving, like alcohol, but it also stays in the body longer than alcohol.

- There is evidence that people become psychologically dependent on cannabis and that it can lead some people to take hard drugs.

Many people campaign for the legalisation of cannabis

Activity

1 Read Romans 13:1–7 on page 83.

2 What does St Paul teach about the authority of the state?

3 How might a Christian apply St Paul's teaching in Romans 13:1–7 to the taking of illegal drugs?

Questions ?

1 What drugs are classed as illegal?

2 Explain the major differences between hard and soft drugs.

3 'Cannabis should be legalised.' Do you agree? Give reasons for your answer, showing that you have thought about more than one point of view.

Attitudes to drugs 1

Jonathan Edwards, Olympic triple jumper

Most Christians are opposed to the use of illegal drugs. Most importantly, perhaps, is St Paul's teaching in 1 Corinthians 3:16–17 that the body is 'God's temple' and that the Holy Spirit from God works within people. St Paul warned that 'if anyone destroys God's temple, God will destroy him. For God's temple is holy, and you yourselves are his temple.' Many Christians would see the use of illegal drugs as going directly against God's wishes for how people should treat their bodies.

Christians are also concerned that the use of illegal drugs can lead people to steal to support their addiction. St Paul instructed that a Christian should not do anything that would cause anyone else to get into trouble. St Paul said:

> The right thing to do is to keep from eating meat, drinking wine, or doing anything else that will make your brother or sister fall. (Romans 14:21)

Many Christian competitors would regard the use of performance enhancing drugs as wrong and a form of cheating. They want to use the talent that God has given them to the glory of God by winning events, and it would seem wrong to be winning when they have taken a harmful substance into their body. Jesus teaches in Matthew 25:14–30 that God has given everyone special skills (talents). Christians believe that they need to discover these skills and use them to serve God.

Jonathan Edwards is a Christian who believes that his talent as a triple jumper gives him an opportunity to show commitment and dedication to God. St Paul told people that if they were to win the prize they must run a straight race.

Adults may legally smoke and drink alcohol in the UK but many Christians believe that alcohol and tobacco should be avoided because of the health risks, not only to themselves but also to others. Also, St Paul taught in Romans 13:13 that Christians must 'behave decently' and 'Do not get drunk with wine, which will only ruin you' (Ephesians 5:18). Some Christians would argue that this means Christians should not drink at all, others argue that this passage teaches Christians not to get drunk.

Different Christian traditions have different perspectives on the use of alcohol and tobacco. Many Quakers advocate total abstinence from smoking and drinking alcohol because of the harm it does to the individual and others. The Salvation Army believes that once people have entered into a relationship with God the life of that person becomes God's. They made total abstinence from alcohol a condition of membership because abstinence rather than moderation seemed to them to be the most effective answer to the

Members of the Salvation Army do not drink alcohol and officers do not smoke

tragedies caused by drunkenness and alcoholism. Salvationists must try to adopt a lifestyle that is beneficial to their well being.

The Salvation Army works to overcome the misery and poverty that results from excessive drinking and feels it would be hypocritical to try to help in such situations unless its own members practised abstinence from that which was the root cause of these problems. The Army wants people to realise that it is not necessary to rely on alcohol to feel confident, communicate with others, or enjoy oneself. The Army also considers tobacco as injurious to health, a waste of money, and a disagreeable thing to inflict on others. For that reason, Salvationists are forbidden to smoke. Salvationists abstain from the non-medical use of drugs or addictive substances.

Many Free Churches such as the Baptists and Methodists use non-alcoholic wine during the services of Holy Communion because alcohol is seen as a cause of many of the evils of modern society. These churches do not want to encourage the use of alcohol.

Questions ?

1 Why might a Christian competitor consider it wrong to take performance enhancing drugs?
2 Explain why Salvationists do not drink alcohol, smoke, or take illegal drugs.
3 What religious teaching might Christians use to oppose the use of drugs?

121

Attitudes to drugs 2

Although some Christian traditions teach abstinence from alcohol, most Catholics and members of the Church of England (Anglicans) would argue that alcohol is acceptable if taken in moderation. They use alcoholic wine during their services of Holy Communion as Jesus used alcoholic wine and it provides a direct link with the Last Supper.

> *Then Jesus took a cup, gave thanks to God, and said, 'Take this and share it among yourselves. I tell you that from now on I will not drink this wine until the Kingdom of God comes.' (Luke 22:17–18)*

Catholics and Anglicans believe that as Jesus and St Paul drank wine then they can do the same. For example, Jesus' first miracle was to turn water into wine during the celebration of the marriage at Cana. However, although these Christians accept the use of alcohol, they do encourage people not to drink to excess.

St Paul never said that people were to give up the drinking of alcohol, only to use it in moderation. For example, he did not tell the deacons not to drink wine, only not to indulge in too much wine (1 Timothy 3:8). He told his friend Timothy that wine could help him overcome illness: 'Do not drink water only, but take a little wine to help your digestion, since you are ill so often.' (1 Timothy 5:23)

Most Christians believe that it is clear, whether or not they drink alcohol or smoke, they have a duty to help those who are addicted to these problems. Many individual Christians give up time to work in centres helping people with drug problems.

Activity

1 Write a description of the miracle at Cana in your own words.

2 Why do you think that many Christians use this miracle to support the drinking of alcohol in moderation?

Questions

1 (a) Why do you think that some Christians use non-alcoholic wine during the service of Holy Communion?

(b) Why do you think other Christians use alcoholic wine during the service of Holy Communion?

2 Why do some Christians believe that it is acceptable to take alcohol in moderation? Support your view with religious teaching.

The wedding in Cana (John 2: 1–10)

Two days later there was a wedding in the town of Cana in Galilee. Jesus' mother was there, and Jesus and his disciples had also been invited to the wedding. When the wine had given out, Jesus' mother said to him, 'They have no wine left.'

'You must not tell me what to do,' Jesus replied. 'My time has not yet come.'

Jesus' mother then told the servants, 'Do whatever he tells you.'

The Jews have rules about ritual washing, and for this purpose six stone water jars were there, each one large enough to hold about a hundred litres. Jesus said to the servants, 'Fill these jars with water.' They filled them to the brim, and then he told them, 'Now draw some water out and take it to the man in

charge of the feast.' They took him the water, which now had turned into wine, and he tasted it. He did not know where this wine had come from (but, of course, the servants who had drawn out the water knew); so he called the bridegroom and said to him, 'Everyone else serves the best wine first, and after the guests have had plenty to drink, he serves the ordinary wine. But you have kept the best wine until now!'

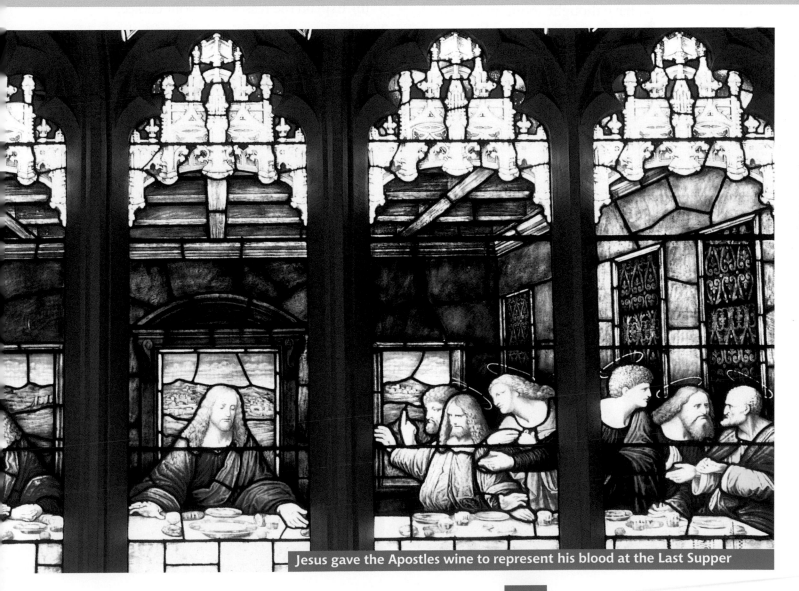

Jesus gave the Apostles wine to represent his blood at the Last Supper

religious attitudes to drug abuse?

Task 1

1 Why might the person in the picture below smoke cigarettes?

2 What other legal drugs might people take?

3 What are the risks to the health of people who take drugs?

4 Explain the differences between hard and soft drugs.

5 What reasons do people give for taking drugs?

6 'What I do with my body is up to me and no one else.' Do you agree? Give reasons for your answer, showing that you have thought about more than one point of view. Refer to religious teaching in your answer.

Task 2

To people who said, 'I am allowed to do anything,' St Paul replied, 'Yes; but not everything is good for you. I could say that I am allowed to do anything, but I am not going to let anything make me its slave.'
(1 Corinthians 6:12)

1 How might Christians apply the words of St Paul to the taking of illegal drugs?

2 (a) What other teachings of St Paul might Christians apply to drug taking?

(b) Explain the reasons for your choice.

3 Why do some Christians work with drug addicts and alcoholics?

Task 3

1 Using the Internet and/or library, find out about the work of an individual or organisation that works to overcome drug problems. For example, David Wilkerson's Christian vocation led him to work with the violent teenage gangs of New York. He succeeded in saving many of them from a life of drug addiction and crime and set up an organisation to help others like them. One of the teenagers that he converted to Christianity, Nicky Cruz, works to help others with drug problems.

2 Write a description of the work of the individual or organisation you have researched.

3 Explain why Christians support work to help people overcome their addiction to drugs or alcohol.

Task 4

'Christians believe that it is wrong to smoke or drink alcohol.' Do you agree? Give reasons for your answer, showing that you have thought about more than one point of view. Refer to religious teaching in your answer.

T.R.U.C.E. (To Reach Urban Children Everywhere) is a Nicky Cruz ministry that tries to persuade at risk teenagers to turn to God

Citizenship Link

The maximum sentence for the possession of Class A drugs is seven years in prison and/or a fine; for Class B drugs, it is five years in prison and/or a fine, and for Class C drugs, two years in prison and/or a fine.

For supplying drugs, the penalties are harsher. The maximum sentence of supplying Class A drugs is life imprisonment and/or a fine; for Class B drugs, it is fourteen years imprisonment and/or a fine, and for Class C drugs, it is five years imprisonment and/or a fine.

1 Do you think it is right that some drugs should carry harsher penalties than others? Give reasons for your answer.

2 Why do you think people who supply drugs receive harsher penalties than people who possess drugs?

3 Do you think that it is right for the suppliers to receive longer sentences? Give reasons for your answer.

Media and technology

The media is the main means of mass communication: it is lots of different ways in which information is passed between people. The forms of media available to most people in the West include:

- newspapers
- magazines
- radio
- television
- cinema
- music
- the Internet
- satellite communications.

Most homes in Britain have at least one radio and television. Over 88 per cent of households have a video recorder and CD player. Over 40 per cent of households have satellite, cable and digital receivers. Over a third of households have Internet access.

Newspapers and magazines are readily available as they are sold everywhere and are cheap to buy. Tabloid newspapers are the most popular form of newspaper, for example *The Sun* and *The Mirror*. A tabloid newspaper has bold headlines, large photographs, and pages half the size of a broadsheet newspaper. Millions more tabloid newspapers are sold

Computers have revolutionised communication

each day than broadsheet newspapers. Broadsheets carry more news and analysis than tabloids and in more detail, for example, *The Telegraph* and *The Guardian*. There are also many magazines available aimed at all ages and interests.

The cinema is another popular form of the media. Most people have access to a cinema in their neighbourhood and going to the cinema has become a popular leisure activity. There were over 142 million admissions to the cinema in the year 2001.

Media and society

Everyone in modern society is affected by the mass media. It is through the different forms of communication that we hear about current events, new products, fashion and entertainment. The media influences what people think, what people buy, what people eat, what people know, and how people dress.

Currently, the average young person spends more than twenty-one hours per week viewing television. This figure does not include time spent watching movies, listening to music, watching music videos, playing video or computer games, or surfing the Internet for recreational purposes. By the time the average teenager leaves school, they will have spent more time watching TV than time studying in the classroom. Children spend more time learning about life through the media than in any other manner. People are divided as to whether the media has benefited society or has harmed it.

Benefits of the media

- It can be used for public information. For example, the drink-driving campaign reduced the number of alcohol associated road deaths.

- Entertainment in the home can be a great advantage to people who are disabled, ill or elderly and unable to get out.

- It gives people knowledge to form and express their own opinions on issues.

- It makes people aware of injustices in the world. For example, the USA was forced to take notice of the civil rights movement because of worldwide pressure to stop the violence against the protestors.

- It makes the world aware of disasters and of ways to help people. For example, the Live Aid concert raised money worldwide to help the starving people of Ethiopia.

- It makes people aware of other cultures and religions in the world and helps to break down barriers of prejudice and discrimination.

The Sun is one of the most popular tabloid newspapers

Activity

In the research activity on page 74 you found out about an organisation that seeks to help overcome the problems of the developing world such as CAFOD or Christian Aid. Find out how the charity you researched uses the media to inform people of its work and to raise funds.

Questions ?

1 What is meant by 'the media'?
2 Name **four** different branches of the media.
3 Why are media and technology linked?
4 What are the main differences between a tabloid and a broadsheet newspaper?
5 What are the influences of the media on society?
6 What are the benefits of the media for the world?
7 How has a charity used the media to support its work?

Concerns about the media

Although the media has brought benefits to society, there are concerns that some of the influences on society have been negative. These concerns about the media influences on society include the following.

- There is concern about the unsupervised availability of television and videos to children. There have been many studies seeking to establish direct links between exposure to film and television and anti-social behaviour. This is often called the 'media effects approach'. It is argued that the increased use of bad language and violence in society is the result of media influences.

- There is also concern that child molesters and paedophiles have used chat rooms on the Internet to get in touch with children by pretending to be the same age and having the same interests.

- Advertising in the media has led people into debt because they purchase products that they cannot afford. At Christmas many children demand presents that their family can ill afford because they have seen the products advertised on television.

- The influence of role models in the media is not always a good one. For example, the media's emphasis on body image is thought to be one of the causes of the increase in the number of people with eating disorders such as anorexia nervosa and bulimia.

- Some people think that the high levels of violence in films, video games and television programmes causes people to be more violent in real life. Some lawyers have tried to use the influence of the media on their client as a defence for the violent crimes their client has committed.

- Many people are concerned that the media includes **obscenity** and as a result encourages immoral attitudes to aspects of contemporary life.

Mary Whitehouse expressed fears about the effects of television in the 1960s. As a Christian, she felt that television was attacking Christian values and undermining family life. In 1964, she set up the National Viewers and Listeners Association. The Association keeps pressure on the Broadcasting Authorities to improve their policies on taste and decency. The Association was founded in the 1960s and it was mainly through their campaigns that the Broadcasting Standards Council (BSC) was set up. After an intensive campaign in 1984 to outlaw 'video nasties', a Private Members' Bill was introduced in Parliament requiring videos to be classified by age suitability in a similar way to films shown at the cinema.

What is...?

Censorship occurs when an official authority examines newspapers, films, television and video, before public release and suppresses any parts on the grounds of obscenity, violence, blasphemy, or a threat to the country's security.

Obscenity refers to something that has the potential to deprave or corrupt.

Questions ?

1 Why are there concerns about the influence of the media?
2 Why do you think that many Christians campaign to limit the influences of the media?

Mary Whitehouse formed The National Viewers and Listeners Association

Does the use of waif-like models cause girls to develop eating disorders?

The most important success of the Association to date is the Protection of Children Act 1978 that made child pornography illegal. This Act enables police action to be taken against those who use the Internet to publish and make available indecent images of children.

The Association presents awards to a broad range of programmes that it considers to have high standards of decency. These have included, *Songs of Praise*, *Blue Peter* and *Holiday*. It has always aimed to praise good programmes and encourage those who make them.

Control of the media

The concerns about media influences have led to various restrictions on what can and cannot be shown in television programmes, films, and sent over the Internet. A restriction on what can and cannot be shown or said is called **censorship**. There are different kinds of restrictions on the media.

- The Obscene Publications Act 1959 and 1964 makes it illegal to publish or send obscene or indecent material.
- The Telecommunications Act 1984 controls what can be said or sent by telecommunications.
- The Post Office Act 1953 controls what can be sent through the post.

Control over broadcasting and newspapers

The television watershed ensures that all television programmes screened in Britain before 9pm are suitable for audiences that include children. The Independent Television Commission (ITC) monitors the independent television companies and deals with complaints. The ITC monitors what is shown by independent television companies and makes sure that the programmes and advertising keeps within the codes and guidelines. The Radio Authority licenses and regulates independent radio services.

Companies spend millions of pounds each year on advertising. The ITC monitors television advertising

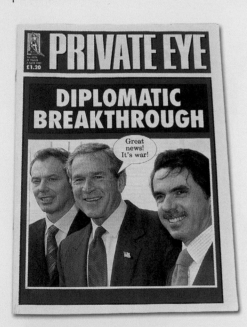

Universal – suitable for all audiences four years and over	Parental Guidance – general viewing, but some scenes may be unsuitable for some children	No one younger than twelve may see a '12A' film at the cinema unless accompanied by an adult. No one younger than twelve may rent or buy a '12'-rated video	No one younger than fifteen may see a '15' film at the cinema. No one younger than fifteen may rent or buy a '15'-rated video	No one younger than eighteen may see an '18' film at the cinema. No one younger than eighteen may rent or buy an '18'-rated video	R18 category is a special and legally restricted classification and may only be supplied in licensed sex shops to people eighteen years and over

The British Board of Film Classification

Advertising on television and radio is required by law to be 'legal, decent, honest and truthful'. The Broadcasting Standards Commission deals with complaints from individuals.

The Internet Watch Foundation monitors the worldwide web and e-mails for potentially illegal items. This includes sites that contain child pornography.

The Press Complaints Commission deals with complaints against the Press. The Commission attempts to prevent the invasion of privacy and has drawn up the Press Code as guidance for journalists working in the media.

Control on films and videos

The British Board of Film Classification classifies by age the suitability of films shown at the cinema and that can be watched and purchased on video. Films have different ratings that restrict access on some films to those under certain ages. Films are rated in the ways according to the amounts of sex and violence in them.

The Video Recording Act 1984 regulated the sale of 'video nasties'. These are video films that included scenes of extreme acts of violence. Many satellite and digital boxes, videos and computers, are now fitted with a parental lock to limit what children can watch without parental supervision.

If the media gets its facts wrong then the individual or organisation might accuse the newspaper or television channel of libel or slander and take them to court.

Question ?

1 What is the television watershed?
2 'I should be able to watch what I want.' Do you agree? Give reasons for your opinion showing that you have thought about more than one point of view.

Freedom of the media

Aled Jones is a regular presenter of *Songs of Praise*

Not everyone agrees with control of the media, as they believe that this limits its freedom to report issues of public interest. Some people doubt that the media has harmful effects and a definite link has never been proven. It has been argued that parents should take responsibility for what their children watch or read and not society as a whole. Individual liberty is restricted by censorship and adults should be able to decide what to watch for themselves.

Many people argue that if there are restrictions on the availability of materials such as pornography, these materials will still be available illegally but it will no longer be possible to monitor them. This will make such materials more dangerous to society.

Another reason for the opposition to censorship is that it could be used to prevent democracy working. If the media presents what the government wants people to know rather than the whole truth then it is difficult for people to make informed decisions.

Religion and the media

Religious broadcasting currently occupies about six and a half hours of broadcasting time each week across the five main TV channels. The BBC is required to broadcast religious programmes because the public pay for the BBC through the TV licence and this means the BBC should provide programmes for all the different groups in society, including religious believers. *Songs of Praise* is the best-known BBC1 religious programme. Radio 4 also broadcasts religious programmes, including *The Daily Service* and *Thought for the Day*. *The Daily Service* on Radio 4 is the longest running radio programme in the world.

Some believers are concerned that whilst the time devoted to religious programmes has remained at similar levels, the scheduling of religious programmes has moved away from peak times and there are fewer programmes broadcasting religious services. The majority of these programmes are Christian but there are programmes related to other religions. For example, during Ramadan there are appropriate religious programmes linked to Islam.

What is...?

An **evangelist** is someone who seeks to spread a religious message to others.

Secular means non-religious.

What do you think? ?

Do you think that parents have the right to control what children over twelve years of age watch? Share your views with your teacher and the rest of the class.

The Religious Broadcasting Act 1990 controls religious broadcasting in Britain and requires the BBC, ITC and the Radio Authority, to ensure that they are responsible not only in terms of providing religious broadcasting, but also that what is broadcast respects the beliefs of listeners and viewers. Programmes must not offend any of the religious views or beliefs of viewers or listeners. All programmes must be accurate and fair and not seek to convert people to a particular belief. The Central Religious Advisory Committee (CRAC) advises the BBC, ITC and Radio Authority about policies and coverage.

Billy Graham has used the media to spread the Christian message since the 1960s

The major religions of the world have recognised the importance of the media as a means of spreading their message throughout the world. The major religions have web sites and e-mail addresses to help people find out more about their faith. Local places of worship will often have their own web page to give details of times of worship and other activities. There are many satellite and digital channels dedicated to the spreading of the religious teachings of a particular faith. This is known as 'televangelism' because people are using the channels to continue the work of **evangelists**.

Many Christians believe that it is acceptable to use the media as a means of spreading the Christian message. The Churches Advisory Council for Local Broadcasting (CACLB) is the Churches organisation for the development, encouragement and promotion of Christian involvement in all aspects of local and regional broadcasting in the UK. CACLB exists to advance the Christian faith through broadcasting. Billy Graham began to use radio broadcasts for his crusades in the 1960s.

Activity

1 Watch a religious broadcast, possibly *Songs of Praise*.

2 Write a review of the programme including reference to the age ranges to which you think it would appeal. Explain in your review why you think it most suitable for that age range(s).

Activity

Find out how Billy Graham has used the media to spread the Christian message.

Questions

1 How might the media be used to spread the Christian message?

2 What are the concerns of some believers about the use of the media for televangelism?

3 'Jesus would have used the media to spread his message if he was preaching today.' Do you agree? Give reasons for your answer, showing that you have thought about more than one point of view.

What do you think?

The debate about the role and purpose of religious broadcasting is not new. Eighty years ago when it was suggested that daily worship should be broadcast on the radio, many clergy rejected the idea for fear that it would be heard in public houses by men wearing hats. Do you think that it matters what a person is wearing if they listen to a religious broadcast? Share your ideas with your teacher and the rest of the class.

Attitudes to media and technology

In the 1980s, preachers moved on to the television, particularly in the USA. These Christians believe that using the media is continuing Jesus' command to 'Go throughout the whole world and preach the gospel to the whole human race' (Mark 16:15).

There is some concern, however, that there have been evangelical Christians in the USA who have used televangelism to make money for themselves and have not led the Christian life that they have been preaching. Jimmy and Tamy Fae Bakker were a prime example of corrupt televangelists who used spiritual guidance as a means of making money for themselves.

As with all moral issues, religious believers use sources of religious authority like sacred texts and religious teachings to decide the attitude they should take to the media and technology. Believers' own consciences also inform their views. Some Christians use St Paul's teaching in 1 Corinthians 5:1–5 that anyone responsible for 'sexual immorality' in the community should be thrown out of the community because they are going against the teachings of God and Jesus. St Paul reminds people that such behaviour is a sin.

In 1 Thessalonians 4:3 St Paul warns people to avoid sexual immorality and 'God wants you to be holy and completely free from sexual immorality'. Some Christians argue that this includes not looking at nudity in the tabloid newspapers or watching sex scenes on film or television, as it is felt that this encourages 'lustful thoughts', which were condemned by Jesus in the Sermon on the Mount.

Christian beliefs have legal protection in this country against **blasphemy**. The last successful prosecution under the law was against the publishers of the magazine *Gay News* in 1977, in connection with a poem depicting Christ as a homosexual.

For some believers, religious teachings are true for all times and people. This is sometimes called a fundamentalist position. Other

Immorality in the Church (1 Corinthians 5:1–5)

Now, it is actually being said that there is sexual immorality among you so terrible that not even the heathen would be guilty of it. I am told that a man is sleeping with his stepmother! How, then, can you be proud? On the contrary, you should be filled with sadness, and the man who has done such a thing should be expelled from your fellowship. And even though I am far away from you in body, still I am there with you in spirit; and as though I were there with you, I have in the name of our Lord Jesus already passed judgement on the man who has done this terrible thing. As you meet together, and I meet with you in my spirit, by the power of our Lord Jesus present with us, you are to hand this man over to Satan for his body to be destroyed, so that his spirit may be saved in the Day of the Lord.

believers may interpret religious teachings for their own times and their views on media and technology to change over time. This is often called a liberal position. Therefore, what many Christians consider blasphemous changes with time. When the musical *Jesus Christ Superstar* opened in London in the 1970s, it was considered inappropriate by many Christians to make a musical of the life of Jesus. Nuns protested alongside other Christians outside the theatre where it was to be shown. Today, most Christians would regard the musical as an appropriate way of using modern technology to spread the message of the meaning of Jesus' death.

There are now several television comedy programmes such as *The Vicar of Dibley* and *Father Ted* that are based around aspects of Christian worship and there are many Christians who watch and enjoy these programmes. A few years ago, many people would have regarded such programmes as blasphemous.

Some Christians considered *Jesus Christ Superstar* blasphemous when it opened

Activity

1 Find out about any aspect of the media that is currently being criticised because it is going to undermine morality or religious beliefs. For example, there may be an advertising campaign that some people find offensive or a storyline in a television soap opera.

2 Outline what you think different Christian responses might be to this case study, supporting your points with reference to religious teaching.

Questions ?

1 What is meant by the term 'blasphemy'?
2 How are fundamentalist Christian views about religious teachings different from those of a liberal Christian?
3 How have attitudes to what is shown on television altered in the last twenty years?
4 'It is not for Christians to tell me what I can watch.' Do you agree? Give reasons for your answer, showing that you have thought about more than one point of view.

religious attitudes to media and technology?

Task 1

1 Explain what the term ' the media' means.
2 How has the media changed in the last 50 years?
3 How does the media influence society?
4 (a) What might be regarded as the benefits the media has brought to society?
  (b) What might be regarded as the harmful effects of the media on society?
5 Outline the different views that Christians might take towards the control of the media and explain why they have those views. Support your points with religious teaching.

Task 2

1 How would you expect *The Mirror* newspaper to be different from *The Independent* in its content and reporting of the news?
2 Explain the concerns that religious people might have about tabloid newspapers.

Task 3

1 What is the main aim of the National Viewers and Listeners Association?
2 Why do you think that many Christians support the aim of this association? Support your answer with religious teaching.
3 Explain why religious people might control the television viewing of their children. Support your answer with religious teaching.

Task 4

The blasphemy laws of Britain only apply to Christianity. Salman Rushdie's novel *The Satanic Verses* (1989) was considered to be blasphemous by most Muslim leaders and was banned in many Islamic countries. The UK law would not allow the prosecution of Salman Rushdie in connection with his novel because it was the Islamic faith and not Christianity that regarded the book as blasphemous, and it was published in Britain. The result was the burning of copies of the book outside several bookshops selling the novel and public protests by Muslims to change the law. The law has not been changed.

1 Why do you think that the blasphemy laws of Britain only apply to Christianity?
2 Many people, including some Christians, argue that the laws should be changed to include those of all faiths or repealed because they are outdated. Do you agree? Give reasons for your answer, showing that you have thought about more than one point of view. Refer to religious teaching in your answer.

The Mirror is a tabloid newspaper and The Independent is a broadsheet

Task 5

'The media ignores people's spiritual needs.' Do you agree? Give reasons for your answer, showing that you have thought about more than one point of view. Refer to religious teaching in your answer.

CNN had live broadcasts from the Gulf War (1991)

Activity

Using the Internet and/or library, choose **one** of the following newspaper stories and write a report of what effect the story has on future events.

- *The Washington Post*'s story in 1972 of the break-in at the Washington headquarters of the Democratic Party (the Watergate building)

- *The Sunday Times*' story in 1972 that thousands of children were born deformed because of a drug called thalidomide

- The media coverage of the failure to fly a flag at half-mast at Buckingham Palace after the death of Princess Diana in 1997

- *The News of the World*'s publication of the names of alleged paedophiles in July 2000.

Citizenship Link

During the Falklands War in 1981, there was a complete news blackout. Every night, John Nott, the government spokesman, gave reports on the war but these reports were censored. The reports only gave what the government wanted people to know. It was felt that it was a matter of national security to limit information about troop movements. It was very difficult for the government to limit information in the Gulf War (1991) as satellite broadcasts gave live coverage of the campaign.

1 What is the term used to describe the limiting of the information given to the general public?

2 What issues do you think the Press should be free to discuss? Give reasons for your answer.

3 What issues do you think the Press should not be allowed to print stories about? Give reasons for your view.

137

The causes of crime

What is...?

A **crime** is an action that breaks the law of the land. Types of crime include:

- crimes against the person such as assault, rape or murder
- crimes against property such as fraud, theft and vandalism
- crimes against the state such as selling secrets to a foreign power (treason).

A **sin** is to break God's laws. Christians regard some crimes such as murder or theft as sins because they break God's commandments not to commit murder or to steal. Other actions may not be a crime under the law but are regarded as a sin by some Christians. For example, adultery is not illegal in Britain but some Christians consider it a sin because it breaks God's commandment, 'Do not commit adultery' (Exodus 20:14).

Activity

1 Read the details of the link between alcohol misuse and crime on page 117.

2 What evidence is there that there is a link between alcohol misuse and crime?

Activity

Protests may turn into riots that break the law. Look back at the causes of riots on page 78. Write a paragraph to explain why people might become involved in a riot.

There is disagreement as to what causes crime. Different points of view include seeing crime as being caused by environmental reasons, social reasons and psychological reasons.

- Statistics show that most people who keep committing crimes (persistent offenders) are also users of hard drugs. Addiction to drugs or gambling has led many people to commit crimes to pay for their addiction.

- Persistent offenders also tend to be unemployed, do not tend to have educational qualifications, and have been in care and are young (under twenty-one). This suggests to some people that environmental reasons are a major cause of crime. These are reasons like poverty, a poor education, and broken homes. Forty per cent of young male prisoners and 30 per cent of young females have been in care.

- One major reason why young people get into trouble and fail to get a good education is truancy. Many offenders have failed to attend school regularly with the result that the literacy and numeracy skills of at least 60 per cent of prisoners are below the average level for an eleven year old. This excludes them from 96 per cent of jobs.

- However, it is not just people from deprived backgrounds that commit crimes and most people who did not have a good upbringing do not necessarily turn into persistent offenders. Boredom causes many acts of vandalism because the individual or group has nothing else to do or peer pressure may persuade an individual to commit a crime to be accepted by the group.

- Some people see psychological reasons as the most important cause of crime. Some psychological problems cause crimes, such as kleptomania (the compulsion to steal) and pyromania (the compulsion to commit arson). Reports estimate that 90 per cent of young people in prison suffer from mental health problems. Some people think crime is caused when people are naturally selfish or greedy.

Criminal responsibility

A child under the age of ten will not be charged with breaking the law. This is because a child under ten is not considered old enough to know right from wrong. It is not until the age of fourteen that a child can be given a custodial sentence such as a detention centre. However, if a child under fourteen does commit a serious crime such as murder, he or she would be held in a place of safety until it was considered there was no longer a danger from the child to

Jamie Bulger disappeared from a shopping centre in Bootle in 1993

society. This is known as being 'held at Her Majesty's pleasure'.
A sixteen year old who breaks the law can be sent to a young
offender's institution and at eighteen can be sent to prison.

Questions ?

1 **(a)** Explain the difference between a crime and a sin.
  (b) State one action that many religious believers regard as a sin
    but is not a crime in Britain.
2 Explain **four** possible causes of crime.
3 What are the links between the misuse of alcohol and crime?
4 At what age is a child responsible for their actions?
5 At what age can a child be sent to a detention centre?
6 At what age can a person be sent to prison?

Activity

1 Find out about the case of the killers
  of Jamie Bulger in 1993.

2 What did the killers defence lawyer
  suggest caused them to commit
  murder?

3 Why do some people think that the
  boys sentenced for the crime have
  the right to privacy now they have
  served their sentence?

4 Why do other people think that the
  Press has the right to inform the
  public of their whereabouts?

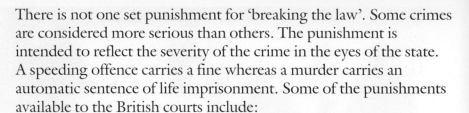

Types of punishment

There is not one set punishment for 'breaking the law'. Some crimes are considered more serious than others. The punishment is intended to reflect the severity of the crime in the eyes of the state. A speeding offence carries a fine whereas a murder carries an automatic sentence of life imprisonment. Some of the punishments available to the British courts include:

- custodial sentences – include imprisonment in adult prison, detention centres or young offender's institutions depending on the age of the offender.

- a community rehabilitation order – involves offenders seeing a probation officer or attending a probation centre on a regular basis. It is hoped that the probation officer can 'advise, assist and befriend' offenders and help them to reform.

- a community punishment order – when the court sets a number of hours (between 40–240 hours) of unpaid work in the community that the offender has to complete as a punishment for their crime. This is sometimes called 'community service'.

- fines – involves the offender having to pay a sum of money to the court as a punishment for their offence.

The five aims of punishment

All punishments seek to reduce the number of crimes committed, but the way that they aim to achieve this varies. There are five main aims of punishment.

- The aim of protection: the punishment is trying to protect society from anti-social behaviour by stopping offenders repeating their actions. A punishment that could be given with the aim of protection is a driving ban for dangerous driving.

- The aim of retribution (revenge): the punishment is intended to pay the offender back for the crime. In the Bible this principle is described as 'an eye for an eye, and a tooth for a tooth'. A punishment with the aim of retribution is prison.

- The aim of deterrence: the punishment seeks to put the offender and others off (deter them from) committing crimes because they do not want to incur the punishment. A punishment for the aim of deterrence is a fine. Seventy-two per cent of all offenders are fined. The number of fines per year would suggest that it is not an effective deterrent.

- The aim of reform: the punishment is devised to help the offender change so that he or she will no longer want to commit future criminal acts. It aims to show offenders that what they did is wrong. A punishment that seeks to reform the offender is a community punishment order.

Activity

Using the Internet and/or library, find out more about the types of punishments available to the courts.

- The aim of vindication: there is no point in having laws unless those breaking the laws are punished. The laws in a society must be respected if they are to work.

What works?

Prisons aim to reduce crime in three ways:

- by deterring potential offenders

- by protecting society by removing offenders from society

- by providing constructive regimes, which encourages prisoners to reform.

Imprisonment may meet the aim of retribution by showing society's attitude to the crime but it does not seem to deter people from committing crimes or to reform them. Over 58 per cent of those discharged from prison are re-convicted within two years. The prison population in England and Wales at the end of April 2001 was 65,800.

Does prison work?

The reasons that prisons do not appear to be working include the following.

- The prison population has increased by 75 per cent over the last ten years. There are insufficient warders to supervise activities so many offenders have to spend up to twenty-three hours a day in their cells. This leads to boredom, resentment, and provides little opportunity to learn skills that could help offenders to get employment when they leave prison.

- Many prisons are outdated and the cells intended for one offender often 'house' up to three offenders. There is evidence that this leads to stress and an increased risk of violence.

- Prisoners learn criminal behaviour from each other. Prisons have been described as the 'universities of crime'. An offender convicted of petty theft often leaves prison with the knowledge of how to commit more serious crimes.

- Imprisonment breaks up families and many offenders have no support or home to go to when they leave prison and end up re-offending.

Questions ?

1 Explain what is involved with each of the following punishments: a driving ban, fine, community punishment order, and imprisonment.

2 **(a)** Explain the five aims of punishment.

(b) For each aim give an example of a punishment that seeks to meet that aim.

3 What evidence is there that fines are not acting as a deterrent?

4 What are the **three** main aims of imprisonment?

5 'Imprisonment fails to meet any of the aims of punishment.' Do you agree? Give reasons for your answer, showing that you have thought about more than one point of view.

Alternatives to prison

Organisations such as NACRO (The National Association for the Care and Resettlement of Offenders) question the effectiveness of prison as the best method of dealing with offenders. It is recognised that society has to be protected from offenders who are a danger to society, but in fact, less than 50 per cent of the offenders in prison have been convicted for violent crimes. Research has highlighted that the chances of rehabilitation are greater the shorter the time an offender is in prison. Long-term sentences can result in offenders becoming institutionalised and unable to cope with a normal day-to-day routine. Three recent initiatives introduced to seek to reduce the number of prisoners who re-offend by helping them to resettle back into the community are:

- the Home Detention Curfew (HDC), which involves selected short-term prisoners spending up to the last two months of their prison sentence subject to an electronically monitored curfew of at least nine hours per day. HDC assists offenders to make the transition from custody to the community. It represents a significant restriction on offender's liberty and places on them the responsibility to comply with their curfew or face being returned to prison.

Electronic tagging is used as an alternative to prison

Activity

Find out about the current work of NACRO (The National Association for the Care and Resettlement of Offenders), which seeks to reform the prison system and to help offenders settle back into the community after imprisonment.

• Electronic tagging is only allowed for offenders with prison sentences of less than four years who are not thought to be a risk to the public, liable to try to escape, or to re-offend. The offender wears an electronic ankle tag and has to remain indoors during the time set. This may be overnight or at a time associated with the crime for which they were convicted.

The parole system is a way of offering a valuable incentive to offenders convicted of more serious crimes to address the root causes of offending behaviour while in prison. The Parole Board assesses the offender's behaviour in prison and their risk of re-offending and if satisfied may release them from prison early. Only around five per cent of those released from prison on parole are recalled for re-offending while on licence.

In 2003, the annual cost per prisoner was £27,500. Organisations such as NACRO argue that there are better and cheaper ways of dealing with offenders. A community rehabilitation order costs on average £1,800 and a community punishment order £1,500. The cost of electronic tagging is about £4 per day. These sentences seem to have greater success in reducing the number of re-offenders and are cheaper.

Capital punishment

When Jesus was crucified there was a sign above his head stating his crime. The main aim of public executions was deterrence. In the case of murder, the death penalty also has the aim of revenge. The offender took a life so his or her life is taken. During the nineteenth century, the death penalty in Britain was mainly used in cases of theft rather than murder. In 1866, public hangings were stopped and replaced by executions within the prison precincts. From 1900 to 1965, there was a growing move to abolish the death penalty and Britain ended the use of capital punishment in 1965. Capital punishment is still used in some states in the USA and many other countries.

There have been arguments about the death penalty being re-introduced into Britain since its abolition. Christians are divided over the issue of capital punishment because it is possible to find biblical teaching to support both points of view.

What do you think? ?

Do you think it is more likely to reduce crime if offenders are kept in the community where possible or will sending all offenders to prison be more effective? Share your thoughts with your teacher and the rest of the class.

What is...?

Capital punishment is the death penalty.

Crucifixion was the form of capital punishment used by the Romans

Activity

Read the views of Christians for and against the death penalty on pages 144–5. Prepare a speech for a class debate on the statement: 'Capital Punishment should be reintroduced into Britain for murder.'

Questions ?

1 (a) Outline the work of NACRO.
  (b) Explain the alternatives to prison that NACRO supports.
  (c) Why does NACRO support these alternative punishments?
2 (a) What is capital punishment?
  (b) What are the **two** aims of capital punishment?

Capital punishment

Activity

Read the extract from Catechism 22:66–7 and complete Task 2 on page 148.

Gary Gilmore was a murderer who asked to be executed rather than spend his life in prison

Activity

Timothy Evans, Derek Bentley and Ruth Ellis were all found guilty of murder and hanged. All three cases contributed to the abolition of capital punishment in Britain. Find out why the death of each of these three people was used to support the abolition of the death penalty.

Arguments for capital punishment

The Catholic Church does accept that the death penalty may be an acceptable form of punishment. Catechism 22:66–7 states that it may be a necessary form of punishment 'in cases of extreme gravity', although in recent months and years Pope John Paul II has asked several heads of state to spare the lives of criminals condemned to death.

Christians in favour of capital punishment might support their views by stating:

- the death penalty acts as a deterrent to murder. Since its abolition, the number of murders and violent crimes has increased significantly.

- the death penalty protects society. It discourages offenders from carrying weapons for fear of using them in the heat of the moment.

- the death penalty removes the risk of the murderer repeating the crime. There have been murderers who have escaped or repeated their crime when freed from prison.

- the death penalty saves money, as society does not have to pay for the offender's upkeep in prison. The money could be used to help those in need.

- some people regard the death sentence as more humane than a life sentence. There are murderers who have requested it (for example, Gary Gilmore in the USA requested that he be executed as he did not want to spend the rest of his life in prison).

- the death penalty is the only punishment that reflects society's horror at certain types of crime. This seems to be supported by the book of Genesis 9:6, which states: 'Human beings were made like God, so whoever murders one of them will be killed by someone else.' The Catholic forum has stated that in many cases, 'the death penalty is sought because of the outrage and pain suffered by the victims and their families', although it also adds that 'we cannot let our emotions determine what is right and what is wrong'.

- the death penalty agrees with the right of revenge given by Moses: 'In such cases show no mercy, the punishment is to be a life for a life, an eye for an eye, a tooth for a tooth, a hand for a hand, and a foot for a foot.'(Deuteronomy 19:21)

Arguments against capital punishment

The General Synod of the Church of England debated capital punishment and passed the resolution that 'This Synod would deplore the re-introduction of capital punishment into the United Kingdom sentencing policy'. The arguments Christians would use against the re-introduction of capital punishment include the following.

- Other people interpret Moses' words to mean that offenders should pay for the value of the life taken, not have their life taken in return. Criminals can be detained in prison for the rest of their lives as an act of vengeance.

- Jesus taught that people should try reform the offender, not seek revenge. Capital punishment removes any chance of reform.

- Quakers (The Society of Friends) oppose capital punishment because of their belief that there is a 'spark of God' within everyone and there must be a reverence for life.

- Execution is a barbaric and outdated practice in modern society. The abolition of the death penalty shows progress towards a civilised society.

- The sixth commandment orders people not to kill, yet society would employ a paid executioner if the death penalty were re-introduced.

- St Paul taught that revenge must be left to God. It is for God to seek vengeance not humans. Humans must seek to forgive and reform the offender.

- A mistake could be made and an innocent person executed for a crime he or she did not commit. There is evidence that this has happened in the past.

- The death penalty punishes not only offenders but also their families because they lose a loved one.

- The death penalty would not stop terrorism. By their actions, terrorists have demonstrated that they are not afraid of dying for their cause. They may welcome the opportunity to become martyrs to the cause.

In conclusion, most people believe that God will forgive the sins of people who are sorry and turn back to him. They believe that they must offer forgiveness to offenders and help them to reform. Society must protect the innocent and punish crimes. Some Christians say that you should hate the sin but love the sinner. Many Christians believe punishments must, in the end, help people to reform and become the person God intended that person to be.

Derek Bentley was sentenced to death after his accomplice shot a policeman during a warehouse burglary

Activity

Read the biblical teaching on pages 147 and 149. Write an explanation of how this teaching might be applied to a Christian's view of capital punishment.

Questions ?

1 Explain why some Christians are in favour of capital punishment. Support your answer with religious teaching.

2 Explain why some Christians are against capital punishment. Support your answer with religious teaching.

Attitudes to capital punishment

Christians do not believe that criminals should go unpunished. Christians agree that society needs to be protected from criminal activities and that the number of crimes committed need to be reduced, but it is the aims behind the punishment that concern Christians. Most Christians believe that Jesus teaches any punishment must not seek revenge but aim to reform the offender. They would want the punishment to show society's disapproval of the crime while seeking to give offenders the chance to change their ways. Christians look at the teaching of Jesus and St Paul as a guide to how offenders should be punished.

Jesus was crucified between two thieves. In the incident of the penitent thief (Luke 23:32–43), one of the thieves is sorry (penitent) for what he has done. He recognises Jesus as the Messiah and asks that Jesus remember him. Jesus answers that he will enter heaven with him. The man is dying but God can still forgive him. The incident would suggest that it is never too late to turn back to God. The criminal recognises Jesus' power to save him from the punishment he deserves for his sins and by turning to Jesus is able to gain forgiveness.

Jesus used parables to teach his followers his message about forgiveness. Two of Jesus' parables, the Parable of the Lost Son and the Parable of the Unmerciful Servant, teach about forgiveness and may be applied to Christian attitudes to punishing offenders.

In the Parable of the Lost Son, the father represents God, and the sons, ordinary people. The teaching is that God is willing to forgive sinners who are sorry and turn back to him and therefore people should be willing to do the same. People must not be like the older brother who refuses to show forgiveness because he thinks he has not done anything wrong. Jesus is teaching that people who are unforgiving are not doing God's will.

Activity

Read the Parable of the Unmerciful Servant on page 149. Complete Task 3 that follows.

Questions ?

1 Explain the views of most Christians towards the aims of punishment.
2 Explain how the incidents of the woman caught in adultery and the penitent thief might influence a Christian's views on punishment.
3 How might the Parable of the Lost Son influence a Christian's views on punishment?

What do you think? ?

Look back at the outline of the incident of the woman caught in adultery (John 8:2–11) that you did for the activity on page 50. How do you think a Christian might apply Jesus' teaching in this incident to the punishment of offenders?

The incident of the penitent thief (Luke 23:32–43)

Two other men, both of them criminals, were also led out to be put to death with Jesus. When they came to the place called 'The Skull', they crucified Jesus there, and the two criminals, one on his right and the other on his left. Jesus said, 'Forgive them, Father! They don't know what they are doing.'

They divided his clothes among themselves by throwing dice. The people stood there watching while the Jewish leaders jeered at him: 'He saved others; let him save himself if he is the Messiah whom God has chosen!'

The soldiers also mocked him: they came up to him and offered him cheap wine, and said, 'Save yourself if you are the king of the Jews!'

Above him were written these words: 'This is the King of the Jews.'

One of the criminals hanging there hurled insults at him: 'Aren't you the Messiah? Save yourself and us!'

The other one, however, rebuked him, saying, 'Don't you fear God? You received the same sentence he did. Ours, however, is only right, because we are getting what we deserve for what we did; but he has done no wrong.' And he said to Jesus, 'Remember me, Jesus, when you come as King!'

Jesus said to him, 'I promise you that today you will be in Paradise with me.'

The Parable of the Lost Son (Luke 15:11–32)

Jesus went on to say, 'There was once a man who had two sons. The younger one said to him, "Father, give me my share of the property now." So the man divided his property between his two sons. After a few days the younger son sold his part of the property and left home with the money. He went to a country far away, where he wasted his money in reckless living. He spent everything he had. Then a severe famine spread over that country, and he was left without a thing. So he went to work for one of the citizens of that country, who sent him out to his farm to take care of the pigs. He wished he could fill himself with the bean pods the pigs ate, but no one gave him anything to eat. At last he came to his senses and said, "All my father's hired workers have more than they can eat, and here I am about to starve! I will get up and go to my father and say Father, I have sinned against God and against you. I am no longer fit to be called your son; treat me as one of your hired workers." So he got up and started back to his father.

'He was still a long way from home when his father saw him; his heart was filled with pity, and he ran, threw his arms round his son, and kissed him. "Father," the son said, "I have sinned against God and against you. I am no longer fit to be called your son." But the father called his servants. "Hurry!" he said. "Bring the best robe and put it on him. Put a ring on his finger and shoes on his feet. Then go and get the prize calf and kill it, and let us celebrate with a feast! For this son of mine was dead, but now he is alive; he was lost, but now he has been found." And so the feasting began.

'In the meantime the elder son was out in the field. On his way back, when he came close to the house, he heard the music and dancing. So he called one of the servants and asked him, "What's going on?" "Your brother has come back home," the servant answered, "and your father has killed the prize calf, because he got him back safe and sound!"

'The elder brother was so angry that he would not go into the house; so his father came out and begged him to come in. But he answered his father, "Look, all these years I have worked for you like a slave, and I have never disobeyed your orders. What have you given me? Not even a goat for me to have a feast with my friends! But this son of yours wasted all your property on prostitutes, and when he comes back home, you kill the prize calf for him!" "My son," the father answered, "you are always here with me, and everything I have is yours. But we had to celebrate and be happy, because your brother was dead, but now he is alive; he was lost, but now he has been found."'

religious attitudes to crime and punishment?

1 State and explain the five aims of punishment.

2 Why do many people believe that prisons are failing to meet these aims?

3 Why do many Christians support the work of organisations such as NACRO? Refer to religious teaching in your answer.

Most prisons were built in the Victorian period

Task 2

Read the extract from Catechism 22:66–7 below and answer the questions that follow.

> *Preserving the common good of society requires rendering the aggressor unable to inflict harm. For this reason, the traditional teaching of the Church has acknowledged as well founded the right and duty of*

One form of capital punishment used in the USA is the electric chair

> *legitimate public authority to punish malefactors by means of penalties commensurate with the gravity of the crime, not excluding, in cases of extreme gravity, the death penalty. If bloodless means are sufficient to defend human lives against any aggressor and protect the public order and the safety of persons, public authority should limit itself to such means.*

1 The electric chair is a form of capital punishment. What is capital punishment?

2 What does the Catechism state is the traditional teaching of the Catholic Church on capital punishment?

3 When does the Catechism state that it is not necessary to use capital punishment?

4 'Capital punishment is less degrading and inhumane than keeping someone locked up in prison for life.' Do you agree? Give reasons for your answer, showing that you have thought about more than one point of view. Refer to religious teaching in your answer.

Task 3

Read the Parable of the Unmerciful Servant opposite and answer the questions that follow.

1 Who do you think the master and the servant represent in this parable?

2 What do you think that this parable teaches about forgiveness?

3 How might Christians apply this teaching to the punishment of offenders?

4 Explain the Christian attitudes to the punishment of offenders. Support your answer with religious teaching.

5 'Christians never break the law.' Do you agree? Give reasons for your answer, showing that you have thought about more than one point of view. Refer to religious teaching in your answer and specific examples.

The Parable of the Unmerciful Servant
(Matthew 18:23–35)

Then Peter came to Jesus and asked, 'Lord, if my brother keeps on sinning against me, how many times do I have to forgive him? Seven times?'

'No, not seven times,' answered Jesus, 'but seventy seven times, because the Kingdom of heaven is like this. Once there was a king who decided to check on his servants' accounts. He had just begun to do so when one of them was brought in who owed him millions of pounds. The servant did not have enough to pay his debt, so the king ordered him to be sold as a slave, with his wife and children and all that he had, in order to pay the debt. The servant fell on his knees before the king. "Be patient with me," he begged, "and I will pay you everything!" The king felt sorry for him so he forgave him and the debt and let him go.

'Then the man went out and met one of his fellow-servants who owed him a few pounds. He grabbed him and started choking him. "Pay back what you owe me!" he said. His fellow-servant fell down and begged him, "Be patient with me, and I will pay you back!" But he refused; instead, he had him thrown into jail until he should pay the debt. When the other servants saw what had happened, they were very upset and went to the king and told him everything. So he called the servant in. "You worthless slave!" he said. "I forgive you the whole amount you owed me, just because you asked me to. You should have had mercy on your fellow-servant, just as I had mercy on you." The king was very angry, and he sent the servant to jail to be punished until he should pay back the whole amount.'

And Jesus concluded, 'This is how my Father in heaven will treat every one of you unless you forgive your brother from your heart.'

Task 4

Universal Declaration of Human Rights

Article 5

No one shall be subject to torture or to cruel, inhumane or degrading treatment or punishment.

Article 6

Everyone has the right to recognition everywhere as a person before law.

Article 7

All are equal before the law and are entitled without any discrimination to equal protection of the law. All are entitled to equal protection against discrimination in violation of this Declaration and against any incitement to such discrimination.

1 How do you think that these articles support the idea of justice under the law?

2 Why do you think that most Christians would agree with these articles?

Citizenship Link

1 How do you think that the concept of justice applies to the punishment of offenders?

2 When sentencing an offender, what factors will the judge or magistrate consider?

3 Why do we have laws, and punishments for breaking the law?

4 Explain why the majority of the population obey the laws.

5 If you had the power:

(a) explain one law you would introduce, with reasons for your choice

(b) explain one law you would abolish, with reasons for your choice.

The scales of justice on top of the Old Bailey, London

The rich in society

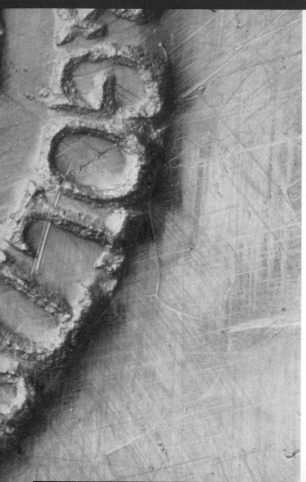

Each year the *Sunday Times* publishes a list of the richest people in Britain. The list includes the Queen, businessmen, pop stars, and writers such as JK Rowling. The ways in which people have become millionaires in Britain include:

- inherited wealth acquired from the estate of someone who has died, usually a relative. Inherited wealth is money that has passed on from one generation to another.

- the receipt of what is called a 'fat cat' salary. This is a term used to describe the salaries of top company executives. The annual salaries and bonuses of these executives may be over £1 million.

- six winning numbers in the National Lottery draw.

The National Lottery is a betting system that raises money for good causes

- creating, inventing or manufacturing something that has sold very well. For example, Bill Gates developed software for personal computers that resulted in the establishment of the very successful Microsoft company and made him very rich.

Bill Gates is estimated to have a personal fortune of £53 billion

Matthew 19:24–30

'I repeat: it is much harder for a rich person to enter the Kingdom of God than for a camel to go through the eye of a needle.'

When the disciples heard this, they were completely amazed. 'Who, then, can be saved?' they asked.

Jesus looked straight at them and answered, 'This is impossible for human beings, but for God everything is possible.'

Then Peter spoke up. 'Look,' he said, 'we have left everything and followed you. What will we have?'

Jesus said to them, 'You can be sure that when the Son of Man sits on his glorious throne in the New Age, then you twelve followers of mine will also sit on thrones, to rule the twelve tribes of Israel. And everyone who has left houses or brothers or sisters or father or mother or children or fields for my sake, will receive a hundred times more and will be given eternal life. But many who now are first will be last, and many who now are last will be first.'

Christian attitudes to wealth

Jesus never said that it was wrong to be rich, only that wealth must not blind people to the needs of others and how God wants them to behave. People who are rich have a duty to share what they have with those who are poor. The Parable of the Sheep and the Goats warns that if rich people are not willing to share then God will condemn them.

In the Sermon on the Mount (Matthew 6:19–24), Jesus warned of the dangers of wealth. Jesus said:

> 'Do not store up riches for yourselves on earth, where moth and rust destroy, and robbers break in and steal. Instead, store up riches for yourselves in heaven, where moth and rust do not destroy, and robbers do not break in and steal. For your heart will always be where your riches are.'

Jesus meant by 'riches' actions of which God would approve such as helping people in need. Jesus said that people cannot 'serve two masters' meaning that people cannot serve both God and money. Jesus meant that the desire to get rich can often blind an individual to the needs of others and so they will not help others less fortunate, as God would wish.

What do you think? ?

It is thought that 'the eye of the needle' was a gate into the walled city of Jerusalem. The goods had to be unloaded from the camel before it could pass through the gate.
What do you think Jesus meant when he said that it was 'much harder for a rich person to enter the Kingdom of God than for a camel to go through the eye of a needle'?

Questions ?

1 Explain different ways by which people may become wealthy.
2 Why might Christians believe that they must use some of their wealth for the good of others? Refer to religious teaching in your answer.
3 What did Jesus warn are the dangers of wealth?

Helping the less fortunate

Many rich people have put the teaching to help the less fortunate into practise. They have established foundations so that some of their wealth is used for good causes. This follows the example of the early church who would 'sell their property and possession, and distribute the money among all, according to what each one needed'(Acts 2:45). An example of such work in contemporary society is the Bill and Melinda Gates Foundation, which is dedicated to improving people's lives by sharing advances in health and learning with the global community.

Most Christians believe that it is better to work hard and earn a living rather than let the money take over a person's life and destroy a person's health. Christians would want that money to be earned honestly and not through any activity that breaks to the law or harms others. There is a fear that wealth might lead to **indolence**.

What do you think?   ?

Look back to the section on poverty in the developing world on pages 72–5. How do you think the teaching of Jesus might be applied to the problems of the developing world?

Does great wealth lead to indolence?

Government action to fight poverty

There are many people in Britain who live below the poverty line. This means that they have barely enough to live on. They live in areas of high crime, bad housing, and have little money for their bills. The government provides the poor with financial support through social security benefits.

Social security is a term used for financial assistance, in whatever form it may take. In Britain, the reasons why financial assistance are given include:

- the relief of poverty

- social protection, not just against poverty from unemployment or low earning, but against hardships if people become sick, to help families with child care and so on

- redistribution of wealth so that the rich provide some support for the poor. Social security is not charity, but is a form of mutual co-operation – a just way of running a society.

Another way by which the government seeks to help the poor is the national minimum wage. This is aimed at providing employees with decent minimum standards and fairness in the workplace. It applies to nearly all workers and sets hourly rates below which pay must not be allowed to fall. The adult rate for workers aged twenty-two and over in 2002 was £4.20 per hour, and the rate for workers aged eighteen to twenty-one in 2002 was £3.60 per hour.

Activity

Look back at the teaching of Jesus' cousin John the Baptist when he taught people to share (Luke 3:10–14), page 72.

Write a paragraph to explain how this teaching might be applied to the treatment of the poor by the rich people in society.

Activity

Find out about the way in which an individual or organisation has used their wealth to help less fortunate people.

What is...?

Indolence is laziness and the wish to avoid activity or exertion. There is a fear that people who do not have to work for their living may become indolent. If people are so wealthy that they do not have to work then there is a risk that they may fill their time with activities that may harm their bodies such as drugs or alcohol.

What do you think? ?

Find out the current minimum wage for workers aged twenty-two and over as well as for workers aged eighteen to twenty-one. Do you think that this is a fair hourly rate? Give reasons for your answer.

Questions ?

1 How does the teaching of John the Baptist apply to helping the poor?
2 How might wealthy people put the teaching of Jesus and John into practise?
3 **(a)** What is meant by 'indolence'?
  (b) Why might Christians be concerned that wealth leads to indolence?
4 **(a)** How does the state seek to protect the poor?
  (b) How is the state's support different from charity?

Unemployment

Technology has reduced the number of employees many firms need

Unemployment exists when someone who wants to work cannot get a job. The person wants to work but is unable to find paid employment. Unemployment is one of the major causes of poverty in Britain because people cannot pay their bills. The causes of unemployment include:

- the product made by a firm is no longer in demand and so the factory has to reduce its workforce because of financial difficulties.

- the introduction of new technology means that a smaller workforce is needed. Robots and machines can now do many jobs. Computers are able to do the work of many people.

- the country's or the world's economy enters a slump and so there is less money to create new jobs.

- people's skills become outdated and are no longer in demand.

- companies employ people for short periods only, rather than permanently.

- the population is rising and there are more people in the country looking for jobs.

The effects of unemployment include:

- there is less money in circulation if there is high unemployment. People buy less and so other shops and factories have to reduce their workforce.

- long-term unemployment can lead to a loss of self-respect. Unemployed people feel of no use to themselves, their family, or society. This can result in depression and even suicide.

- the divorce rate increases as unemployment may lead to friction between couples. This could be the result of mounting debts, irritability because of the unemployed person's frustration at not getting a job, or that the unemployed person is always at home.

- an increase in crime is linked to unemployment. Vandalism is one way in which the unemployed takes out their frustration on a society that has failed to give them a job. The lack of a regular income leads people to steal to pay their debts.

- there is less income tax available to spend on the National Health Service and education. This is because fewer people are paying tax and more people are receiving benefits.

Christians believe that they should help the unemployed. This may be by providing help in the form of luncheon clubs for the unemployed or holidays for their children. It could involve setting up training programmes so that the unemployed can learn a new skill. Many Christians believe the Church has a duty to put political pressure on the government to give financial support to British industry to help with the creation of more jobs.

Homelessness

One result of poverty is homelessness. Many people end up sleeping on the streets, in bed-and-breakfast accommodation, or hostels because they cannot afford a place of their own. People without a home find it difficult to get a job or social security because they have no permanent address at which they can be contacted. People without a steady income find it difficult to afford a place of their own. Homeless people have a right to be housed by their local authority who will pay for bed-and-breakfast accommodation. There are also lists for housing, which homeless people can join. There are many reasons why young people become homeless including:

- problems at home such as not getting on with their parents, violence or sexual abuse

- problems in care such as bullying, being fed up with being in care, or not being involved in decisions about their future

- problems at school such as bullying or playing truant and frightened that their parents will find out

- addiction to drugs or alcohol.

Activity

1 Look back at the causes of crime on page 138.

2 What causes of crime might be linked with unemployment?

Many poor people are homeless and sleep on the streets each night

Questions ?

1 What is unemployment?
2 Explain **three** causes of unemployment.
3 Explain **three** effects of unemployment.
4 Why do you think that Christians believe that they have a duty to help the unemployed? Support your answer with biblical teaching you have studied.
5 How could the following help to overcome the problems of unemployment?
  (a) An individual.
  (b) The Church.
6 'If people are homeless it is their own fault.' Do you agree? Give reasons for your answer, showing that you have thought about more than one point of view.

Attitudes to poverty

The Salvation Army is a Christian tradition that believes that they must put their faith into action by helping those in need. Since its foundation by the Reverend William Booth in 1865, it has become the largest voluntary social work agency in the world. The Salvation Army helps the homeless and the Salvation Army Housing Association provides housing for single people in need of housing. Food is taken out to the homeless sleeping on the streets in major cities each night and 3,250 beds are provided for homeless people every night. At any one time, a further 1,600 people are living in Salvation Army resettlement programmes.

The Salvation Army helps over 300 runaway children each year, many of whom become homeless. An example of a Salvation Army project to help the homeless exists in Oxford. Salvationists make contact with rough sleepers in and around Oxford, and provide them with information, advice, encouragement and support, to help them find accommodation.

Use the Internet and/or library to find out more about how the Salvation Army helps the homeless.

Two hundred years ago many people thought that the rich deserved to be rich because they worked hard. The poor, it was thought, could stop being poor if they worked hard, stayed away from alcohol and gambling, and behaved decently and respectfully. Today, some people still hold this kind of view. Other people, however, think that society has a responsibility to help those who are living in poverty. Religious traditions are very involved in helping combat poverty, whether in this country or abroad. Religious organisations often have a very important role in local communities, organising food for the homeless and services, and support for the unemployed and those below the poverty line. This is because religious traditions believe that God wishes people to help those worse off than themselves.

Christians are taught that they must help the poor and that the poor are just as important as the rich. Jesus taught that the poor had special favour with God. In the Sermon on the Mount, Jesus said: 'Blessed are you who are poor, for yours is the kingdom of heaven.'

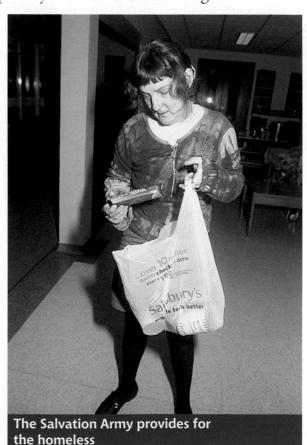

The Salvation Army provides for the homeless

Questions ?

1 Why do people become homeless?
2 Why might Christians feel that they should help the homeless?
3 Describe the work of an organisation that seeks to help the homeless.
4 Why do you think that Jesus taught that acts of charity should be in secret?

What do you think? ?

Look back to Matthew 6:1–4 on pages 72–3. Jesus taught that it is very important that any charity given to help the needy must be from a genuine desire to help rather than to get public acclaim.
Do you think that there are some famous people who give wealth to charities in public to increase their fame?
What do you think might have been the view of Jesus to such gifts of charity? Share your view with your teacher and the rest of the class.

The National Lottery

The Lottery has given many people hope that they could become rich. The aim of the National Lottery is to support good causes. Twenty-eight pence of every £1 spent on a lottery ticket goes to good causes in Britain. The money raised includes support for: the Arts; sport; National heritage, which includes historic buildings, cultural events and so on; and charities.

Christian attitudes to gambling

Most Christians believe that people's lives are in God's hands. As gambling is based on luck and chance, many Christians believe that it contradicts this belief. They are concerned that gambling can be addictive and can cause misery and poverty to the families of those caught in its web. Addiction to gambling can be a cause of crime as the addict steals to support their habit, convinced that they will have a big win that will solve all their problems. Many Christians are also unhappy that in any form of gambling, people are making gain through other people's loss, the principle on which gambling operates. Some Christians such as Salvationists and Methodists, when asked to support a lottery or raffle in aid of charity, would prefer to support the cause by making a donation instead. Many Christians would prefer to work for charities that seek to help the poor.

Some Christians believe that the damage that the National Lottery could do society by encouraging gambling outweighs the advantages of the money raised for good causes. These Christians argue that Jesus taught people to put their trust in God and not worry about their income. In the Sermon on the Mount (Matthew 6:25–34), Jesus told people not to worry about whether they have food or clothes, as God will care for them. Jesus taught that it is more important to try to live a life that follows God's laws.

St Paul warned his friend Timothy that the desire for wealth can be dangerous as the love of money can be at the root of evil actions. For example, the desire to get rich leads people to gamble or to commit crimes. St Paul said that:

But those who want to get rich fall into temptation and are caught in the trap of many foolish and harmful desires, which pull them down to ruin and destruction. For the love of money is a source of all kinds of evil. Some have been so eager to have it that they have wandered away from the faith and have broken their hearts with many sorrows.' (Timothy 6:9–10)

Lotto Draw

Wed 08 Jan 2003 – Draw 735 Bonus

10 12 22 34 46 48 03

A £3m Jackpot

Machine: LANCELOT		Ball Set: 8
Balls matched	How many winners	How much won
6	6	£557,774
5 + Bonus	11	£93,612
5	487	£1,321
4	17,833	£79
3	323,125	£10

Lotto Draw

Sat 11 Jan 2003 – Draw 736 Bonus

09 18 22 26 37 41 20

A £5.5m Jackpot

Machine: GALAHAD		Ball Set: 7
Balls matched	How many winners	How much won
6	3	£1,900,095
5 + Bonus	14	£125,281
5	724	£1,514
4	37,387	£64
3	673,089	£10

Questions ?

1 **(a)** What is the National Lottery?
  (b) What is the aim of the National Lottery?
2 Why do many Christians express concern about the National Lottery?
3 Why might other Christians think that the National Lottery is a good idea?
4 Why might many Christians think that 'the love of money is a source of all kinds of evil'?
5 Explain why many Christians support the work of charities that exist to tackle poverty.

religious attitudes to rich and poor in society?

Task 1

Read the Parable of the Rich Man and Lazarus (Luke 16:19–31) opposite and answer the questions that follow.

1 Why did the rich man find himself in Hades?

2 Where was the rich man told that he had been warned of the dangers of ignoring the needy?

3 What might the Parable of the Rich Man and Lazarus teach rich people in modern society about the use of their wealth?

Task 2

1 Read the Parable of the Rich Fool (Luke 12:13–21) on page 73.

2 The rich fool's wealth would be inherited by someone who had not earned it. Explain the problems that might be faced by someone who suddenly becomes very rich.

3 Explain Christian attitudes to wealth and possessions.

'I will tear down my barns and build bigger ones, and there I will store all my grain and my goods.' (Luke 12:13–21)

Task 3

The early Church shared what they had, as the incident of Barnabas and the early Church demonstrates. Read the incident opposite and explain how Christians might believe that they can follow the example of the early Church in modern society.

Task 4

'It is wrong for a few people to be multi-millionaires while other people live on the streets.' Do you agree?

Give reasons for your answer, showing that you have thought about more than one point of view. Refer to religious teaching in your answer.

Citizenship Link

Read the following articles from the Universal Declaration of Human Rights and write a report to explain how these articles apply to the distribution of wealth in society.

Universal Declaration of Human Rights

Article 17

1 Everyone has the right to own property alone as well as in association with others.

2 No one shall be arbitrarily deprived of his property.

The Rich Man and Lazarus (Luke 16:19–31)

There was once a rich man who dressed in the most expensive clothes and lived in great luxury every day. There was also a poor man named Lazarus, covered with sores, who used to be brought to the rich man's door, hoping to eat the bits of food that fell from the rich man's table. Even the dogs would come and lick his sores.

'The poor man died and was carried by the angels to sit beside Abraham at the feast in heaven. The rich man died and was buried, and in Hades, where he was in great pain, he looked up and saw Abraham, far away, with Lazarus at his side. So he called out, "Father Abraham! Take pity on me, send Lazarus to dip his finger in some water and cool my tongue, because I am in great pain in this fire!"

'But Abraham said, "Remember, my son, that in your lifetime you were given all the good things, while Lazarus got all the bad things. But now he is enjoying himself here, while you are in pain. Besides all that, there is a deep pit lying between us, so that those who want to cross over from here to you cannot do so, nor can anyone cross over to us from where you are." The rich man said, "Then I beg you, father Abraham, send Lazarus to my father's house, where I have five brothers. Let him go and warn them so that they, at least, will not come to this place of pain."

'Abraham said, "Your brothers have Moses and the prophets to warn them; your brothers should listen to what they say." The rich man answered, "That is not enough, father Abraham! But if someone were to rise from death and go to them, they would turn from their sins." But Abraham said, "If they will not listen to Moses and the prophets, they will not be convinced even if someone were to rise from death."'

The believers share their possessions (Acts 4:32–37)

The group of believers was one in mind and heart. None of them said that any of their belongings were their own, but they all shared with one another everything they had. With great power the apostles gave witness to the resurrection of the Lord Jesus, and God poured rich blessings on them all. There was no one in the group who was in need. Those who owned fields or houses would sell them, bring the money received from the sale, and hand it over to the apostles; and the money was distributed to each one according to his need.

And so it was that Joseph, a Levite born in Cyprus, whom the apostles called Barnabas (which means 'One who Encourages), sold a field he owned, brought the money, and handed it over to the apostles.

Article 22

Everyone, as a member of society, has the right to social security and is entitled to realisation, through national effort and international co-operation and in accordance with the organisation and resources of each state, of the economic, social and cultural rights indispensable for his dignity and the free development of his personality.

Article 23

1 Everyone has the right to work, to free choice of employment, to just and favourable remuneration ensuring for himself and his family an existence worthy of human dignity, and supplemental, if necessary, by other means of social protection.

2 Everyone, without any discrimination, has the right to equal pay for equal work.

Preparing for the examination

Look for clues in the examination question

There are often clues in the words used in the questions to indicate what the examiner is looking for in your answer.

'Describe' is asking you for a detailed account of something. For example, if the question asks you to **'Describe** a situation in which one religious tradition might agree with the ending of life,' you need to show that you know that for some believers there are situations when they might think an abortion or euthanasia is the more loving action.

'In what ways' is a phrase used to test your knowledge of religious beliefs or practices. For example, if the question asks, **'In what ways** is the environment being harmed?' then you need to show that you know several causes of damage to the environment.

'Give or state' wants you to present briefly the information that is requested in the question.

'Tell in your own words' is asking you to write an account, usually of an incident or teaching (without having to quote the text at length). For example, you might be asked to **'Tell in your own words** a religious story that teaches the importance of helping the poor', such as the Parable of the Sheep and the Goats.

'Explain' is asking you to interpret or to give reasons for something. For example, **'Explain** the term "sanctity of life"' is asking you to show that you understand the term 'sanctity of life' by explaining the term in your own words.

'Give the meaning of' or **'What is meant by…?'** are phrases to test your understanding of specialist words, phrases or concepts. For example, **'What is meant by** conscience?' is asking you to show that you understand the concept of conscience by explaining what the word means.

An evaluation question will usually have a statement followed by, **'Do you agree? Give reasons for you answer, showing that you have thought about more than one point of view.'** You need to show in your answer the different religious viewpoints related to the statement and evidence to support these different opinions. Then you need to show the examiner **how far you agree** with the statement given and why you hold this opinion. In your answer you must include some religious teachings and writings to support the different religious viewpoints.